T0198727

ELEVATING
CEO
CONSCIOUSNESS

6 STEPS
FOR LEADERSHIP
IN THE STORM

MARC-ANTOINE TSCHOPP

BALBOA.PRESS
A DIVISION OF HAY HOUSE

Balboa Press books may be ordered through booksellers or by contacting:

Balboa Press
A Division of Hay House
1663 Liberty Drive
Bloomington, IN 47403
www.balboapress.com
844-682-1282

Because of the dynamic nature of the Internet, any web addresses or links contained in this book may have changed since publication and may no longer be valid. The views expressed in this work are solely those of the author and do not necessarily reflect the views of the publisher, and the publisher hereby disclaims any responsibility for them.

The author of this book does not dispense medical advice or prescribe the use of any technique as a form of treatment for physical, emotional, or medical problems without the advice of a physician, either directly or indirectly. The intent of the author is only to offer information of a general nature to help you in your quest for emotional and spiritual well-being. In the event you use any of the information in this book for yourself, which is your constitutional right, the author and the publisher assume no responsibility for your actions.

Any people depicted in stock imagery provided by Getty Images are models, and such images are being used for illustrative purposes only. Certain stock imagery © Getty Images.

Print information available on the last page.

ISBN: 979-8-7652-4001-4 (sc)
ISBN: 979-8-7652-4003-8 (hc)
ISBN: 979-8-7652-4002-1 (e)

Library of Congress Control Number: 2023905555

Balboa Press rev. date: 03/30/2023

CONTENTS

Foreword by Om Swami ix

Acknowledgment xv

Introduction xix

The Storm 1

    There is No Such Thing as Chance 3

    Look Below The Surface 8

The Paths 13

    Survive or Die 15

        Body, Mind, and Something Else 17

        The Four Human Qualities 19

        Our Friend Ego 21

        When There is Not Enough 28

    Grow in the Unknown 30

        Once You Achieve Money and Fame 36

        How Much is Enough? 38

        Trust Your Little Prince 40

        What If There is Enough? 43

The Map 45

    The Ten Survival Strategies 49

        Flight 51

        Fight 52

        Freeze 54

        Pro-Create 56

        Seduce 57

        Letting Ourselves Be Seduced 58

Protect 59

Letting Ourselves Be Protected...............................61

Dictate 63

Play The Victim 65

The Ten Strategies to Grow Abundance 67

Humor 69

Sympathize..72

Compromise..73

Trust..75

Play 78

Empathize 82

Co-create...84

Forgive...87

Express Gratitude 89

Be compassionate...90

The Compass **93**

1ˢᵗ Step: PAUSE...95

Stay Silent...97

Breathe 99

Take A Step Back...103

It Is Never Against You 105

2ⁿᵈ Step: OBSERVE 107

Observe Your Physical Feelings 108

Guided Meditation For Observing Our Physical

Sensations 109

Observe Our Emotions...112

Name Your Emotion...115

Understand Your Emotions..................................120

Face Your Fear..122

Be Kind With Your Anger 125

Assess Your Hidden Anger...................................126

Mirror Your Anger 128

Be Smart...129

Tame Your Moods..132

Observe Your Thoughts.......................................135

Practice Mindfulness..137
Identify The Stories We Tell Ourselves About Ourselves......139
3rd Step: DECIDE..142
You Always Have The Ability To Respond.......................144
Be Consistent With Yourself 149
Trust Your Gut 152
Know How To Discern...153

The True North..155

4th Step: LOVE YOURSELF FIRST....................................157
Find Your Masters..161
Honor Your Ancestors 164
Make Friend with Death...165
Express Your Purpose 167
Your Strengths Are Your Values.................................170
Your Superpowers Lie In Your Wounds 174
Your Needs Are Your Priorities.................................175
Self-Compassion Is Your Philosophy.............................177
5th Step: RESPECT YOUR RELATIONSHIPS............................179
Strengthen Your Happiness......................................183
Give Your Trust First..185
Smile Authentically 189
Communicate Unconditionally 191
Use Conflicts To Grow..194
Seek True Encounters...199
6th Step: EXPECT NOTHING IN RETURN..............................202
Detach, Nothing is Permanent...................................208
Unload Your Backpack...213
Practice Tough Compassion......................................217

Conclusion 221

FOREWORD

BY OM SWAMI

On the journey of life, we meet numerous co-travelers. And every person we meet has hopes, dreams, ambitions, and stories hiding in their hearts like warmth in ember. But we don't remember all of them. In fact, only a handful of people make an indelible impression on our minds. Marc-Antoine Tschopp, or MAT as we call him lovingly, is one such person for me.

In the last three decades, I have had the good fortune of meeting some truly remarkable people. From billionaires to the most erudite scholars and teachers, from world-class athletes to amazing writers, and I learned something from each of them. However, my first impression when I met MAT in 2015 was a different story. Here was a wonderful person, a successful entrepreneur, a life coach, but he carried and exuded zen-like serenity. The kind that comes from a person who is no longer anxious about things beyond our control, the type that comes from the one who is in harmony with the world around him. And there is much to be learned from such people. For, there are a million books out there that can give you all kinds of information, but only a few speak from genuine experience.

Elevating CEO Consciousness is one such book. It is full of great insight to help anyone master and apply the art of leadership not only in business but in all aspects of their lives.

Going back to my first meeting with MAT, I remember a particular visual where he was sitting quietly bathing in the warm winter sun in the Himalayan mountains (that's where I live) unaffected by the lack of amenities due to the remoteness of the place. In my humble opinion, someone operating with a higher level of CEO Consciousness must have that serenity of mind. The storms will be raging around you, but that doesn't mean the rage should storm out of you to deal with the challenges. For, a great CEO is not someone who's always screaming on the field like a worked-up football coach but also bonding with his team in silence back in the dressing room.

And that's precisely where MAT does an excellent job in *Elevating CEO Consciousness*. He goes to the root of the issue: your mind, your consciousness. Sharing interesting lessons, he makes this heady cocktail mixing his own experiences with a wide array of philosophies—both from the East and the West—offering us a truly holistic view of leadership.

As Bear Grylls says in *If I Could Tell You Just One Thing*:

> *It is not the most masculine, macho, or the ones with the biggest muscles who win. It's those who look after each other, who remain cheerful in adversity, who are kind and persistent and positive. These are the characteristics that help you, not just to survive life but to enjoy it. The people who are successful are the ordinary ones that just go that little bit further, who give a little more than they are asked to, who live within that extra five percent.*

While each one of us has to walk our own path and arrive at the truth in our manner, *Elevating CEO Consciousness* does a wonderful job of carving out a path for the reader. MAT doesn't just go a little bit further but a lot further than most authors I've read. At times, you will feel like you are reading a deep work of philosophy.

The storm, the paths, the map, the compass, and the true north. He has simplified the whole journey and art of leadership covering strategies and enhancing the fundamental idea of being mindful and thriving in a constant flow of awareness.

What I find beautiful about MAT and his book is that it is not just the message but the messenger too is grounded in reality and truth.

It is, perhaps, why I could not say no to writing a foreword for him and I'm mighty glad that I didn't say no. After all, what could possibly be more joyous than the feeling that you've done your two cents' worth to make this world a better place, to make a difference in someone's life? That's exactly what MAT and his work stand for: making a positive difference in the lives of others. So, "no" wasn't an option. The readers— who may or may not be CEOs— that will benefit from this read and resultantly run more purposeful and meaningful organizations is potent enough a cause that warrants nothing else but a yes.

This book is unique in ways more than one. If you are pressed for time, you can just randomly open any page and give it a go and in great likelihood, you will walk away with an insight.

I hope you enjoy and gain from this read tremendously and go on to do beautiful things with your blessed lives.

Peace
Om Swami
10-02-2023

ACKNOWLEDGMENT

We must find time to stop and thank the people who make a difference in our lives.

—John F. Kennedy

I am just a channel. Everything I have learned, I have received freely from loved ones.

My laboratory is within my little family. Patricia, Illona, Leandro, Shiatsu, Lola, Inka, Milo, Baghi, the Cardinal and Jaya have given me the most intense lessons.

My imprints were passed on to me by my ancestors, my parents, my brothers, my sister and the animals that accompanied my childhood.

My motivations came from committed dreamers: John Lennon, Mohamed Ali, Martin Luther King, Gandhi, Einstein, Cat Stevens, Aldous Huxley, Ernesto Guevara, Carlos Castaneda, Charles Bukowski, Nelson Mandela, Paulo Cuelho, and many friends who crossed my path.

My knowledge was given by Carl Gustav Jung, Jean Piaget, Richard Moss, Heidi Schleifer, Olivier Clerc, Swamy Parthasarathy, Alberto Villoldo, and many others.

My wisdom was sharpened by the radiance of Padre Pio, Satya Narayan Goenka, Don Miguel Ruiz, Mata Amritanandamayi, Avdhoot Shivanand Ji, Dadi Janki, Pope Francis, Jaggi Vasudev and Om Swami.

This book was made possible by the gifts of my coachees and the collaboration of my editors.

I express my deepest and humblest gratitude to all of them: "thank you, Thank you, THANK YOU."

INTRODUCTION

Somewhere beyond right and wrong, there is a garden.
I will meet you there.

— Jalal Ad-Din Rumi

Selim leans forward in his chair, his expression heavy with grief. "More than fifty thousand dead and twenty four million people affected in the space of a few minutes, it is hardly believable. What a tragedy for these Turkish and Syrian families, as if they didn't have enough suffering already," he shares with me as we begin our session.

I can't help but feel the weight of his words as memories flood my mind. Memories of my recent stay in Istanbul. Memories of the tourists from all over the world who, with me, were waiting in the long queue to enter the Hagia Sophia. Memories of the boats that transited between east and west, filled with Ukrainian foodstuffs. Memories of the Çamlica Camii, a huge complex worthy of a sixteenth-century Ottoman emperor, recently built in honor of the influential leader of the moment and supposed to accommodate a hundred thousand people in case of an earthquake. Unfortunately, it is too far for these refugees.

I could bounce off Selim's comment and bemoan the egos of those politicians who run countries and seem to abuse their power, but I know he doesn't appreciate those who feed on unpleasant emotions. Neuroticism is not one of his personality traits.

Selim is conscientious. He must run his business and doesn't have time to think about how to impress his opponents by showing that he is the strongest. This morning, he has to let go of a 60-year-old executive. He is putting the brakes on the growth strategy he sold to his shareholders and his teams. Selim knows he must do it, but it pains him greatly because he has known this employee for over 20 years.

He is quick to reason. He serves the common good, and that means firmness and courage. Yesterday, he was working on the fears of recession and the drain of resources due to the great resignation. The day before yesterday, it was the new disrupters and the war for talent. Tomorrow morning, it will be AI solutions and the repositioning of his core business.

He's running. It excites him, and he feels useful. Complacent smiles give him plenty of attention to remind him of his importance. Inspiring, listening, thinking, and deciding are the fuels that keep him going.

But for some time now, he has found himself doubting. One of his close friends died suddenly at the age of 45. He was athletic and ate well. He also ran. His two young children did not have time to discover what a wonderful person he was.

Although he impressed his world with his confidence, he no longer really recognized himself in his role. At night, alone in his hotel room, Selim wonders if he is really doing the right thing. He feels tired and has trouble looking at himself in the mirror. This race seems never-ending. The acronym VUCAEST (VUCA was coined in 1987, based on the leadership theories of Warren Bennis and Burt Nanus to describe or reflect on the volatility, uncertainty, complexity and ambiguity of general conditions and situations) has just been revealed to him. It is true that everything becomes more Erratic, Speedy, and Turbulent.

He needs to find his flame and asks me: "Are you sure that humans are as good as you claim?"

"Why are you asking me this question?" I reply.

"Because it's hard to be good when I'm about to fire someone and especially because I think we are born pure and innocent, but we become selfish, violent, and immoral with time."

This is a valid observation, and the question needs clarification. For whom is it necessary to be good? Myself, the one who disturbs others or those who want to move forward? And how can we evaluate what is the right thing to do? It addresses a fundamental theme. The kind we ask ourselves when we are torn between satisfying physical and psychological desires or serving environmental and spiritual causes.

I was only four years old when JFK was assassinated, six years old for Malcolm X, and nine years old for Martin Luther King Jr., yet I still remember those black-and-white images my father watched on television. I also remember the demonstrators who put flowers on the end of police guns to demand peace in Vietnam, the students who flipped cars in the streets of Paris, and the monks who set themselves on fire to show their disagreement. There were also Neil Armstrong and Buzz Aldrin happily jumping on the moon, and thousands of half-naked youths rolling around in the mud at Woodstock. I could immediately tell the difference between what was right and what was wrong.

But the older I got, the more complicated that distinction became. The Concorde flew from Paris to New York in three hours but consumed two hundred fourty tons of fuel per trip. PCs and the internet became available to everyone, but interpersonal communication became poorer. The Berlin Wall and the Cold War fell, but ethnic and economic wars increased tenfold. Medicines spread, but diseases became more complex. Access to the stock market was democratized, but financial crises increased. Amazon was created and small retailers disappeared. Facebook brought us closer and voters were manipulated. The World Trade Center towers fell and axes of evil were fought on the other side of the globe. A black president was elected in the US and Snowden revealed secrets. Russia annexed Crimea and Trump made friends with Kim Jong-un. The masks of COVID dissipated in joy as the Iranian chādors flew away in terror. The fight against global warming preoccupied decision-makers for a decade, but every year brought new heat records. The Kremlin bear wanted to reclaim his former empire, and a comedian received billions to counter him.

Selim has to make crucial decisions and wants to regain the enthusiasm that inspired many talents to follow him. He shares with me a definition of intelligence: the ability to adapt to a new situation, understand and solve specific difficulties, make sense of the events around us, and act with discernment, and says: "I understand these words. I can think well and have learned to manage my emotions, but that's no longer enough to know what to do in this turmoil."

I agree with him, we need to develop the attitude of the wise, those who call upon intelligence that is free from the influence of our biological body and unconscious psychology, those who connect to their true self, the source of who we are. We must become conscious leaders to inspire those young talents who have lost faith in our economic and political systems.

This book is the result of twenty five years of research and trials. It guides you to increase your leadership and impact in a world that is losing its bearings. I intend to prepare you to be a conscious, authentic, and successful leader who seizes the opportunities that storms bring. Someone who remains calm and perceives subtle information to build discernment. Someone who listens to his consciousness to make tough and compassionate decisions for all stakeholders.

The stories are true. I have only changed the names and specific details to protect the privacy of the protagonists. I aim to share simple tools that have helped thousands of C-Suite Executives make their best decisions confidently. It will not only help you win hearts and minds during board meetings and complex negotiations but also help you find serenity outside of the workplace.

You can follow my proposed structure or use the table of contents to pick a theme that appeals to you.

Chapter 1 illustrates the kind of storms we are facing.

In Chapter 2, we explore the two mindsets. They are the paths that open before us whenever the storm arrives: we either close in on ourselves and our fellow human beings or open up to everything that's around us and experience true abundance.

Like any navigator sailing into unfamiliar waters, you need a map, a compass, and a true north to steer by, and I have them for you.

Chapter 3 will give you the map of human relationships. You will discover the nineteen strategies we use to deal with new challenges, often unconsciously.

Chapter 4 will provide you with a simple compass that you can use in any situation at any time.

Chapter 5 will help you define your true north, the one within you, the one that makes you unique and powerful, the one that's aligned with your purpose and values, and the one that will allow you to remain serene and joyful as you face every new encounter with clarity and without fear.

THE STORM

There is No Such Thing as Chance

When I went to school, they asked me what I wanted to be when I grew up. I said, "Happy." They told me I didn't understand the question. I told them they didn't understand life.

— John Lennon

It's a sunny morning, and the smiling voice of Johnny Clegg, 'the White Zulu,' fills my car. I feel proud and important.

Daniel, the new CEO of Darewest, had warned me how COVID had made underlying problems surface at the company. The previous management team's plans had been too ambitious, the group had been drowning in debt, and the balance sheet needed a fast fix. Calm, introverted, results-oriented, and detail-minded, Daniel knew what to do. A third of his 1,200 employees would have to go. It was a painful ordeal. Darewest had employed generations of the same families in this poor region for a hundred years or more. The company had underpinned the whole community, but what other choice did Daniel have?

Now, eighteen months later, they still need help. Used to working under paternalistic and directive leadership, many of its longer-serving managers cannot accept the responsibility of making difficult but necessary decisions. Employees, middle management, and some EXCO members have lost confidence, and key people are leaving. Recruiting the right talent is difficult.

They need a savior, so today, I'm going to sit down with their leadership team, suggest ways to put their traumatic past behind them and help them regain the commitment they need from their workforce. But this inner savior of mine is different from the one from my early years. Today I know he is just an actor in a play called Darewest. I must play this part to the fullest, without fear of fluffing my lines and with the confidence to share my truth.

There is no such thing as chance... and I am not here by chance. My presence is the culmination of all my previous actions. My role is to encourage the leadership team to express the hidden truth because others haven't done so before. It's as simple as that. I want them to see that they can choose to play their roles too and not allow fear, anger, sadness, guilt, or shame to decide their futures.

Looking back on my past experiences, I see many such moments of "truth." They never happened by chance, and they always brought me essential gifts, even if I didn't see them as such at the time.

I settled back into the Swiss Mountains for the first time in months. Big, gentle snowflakes drifted down, deepening an already pleasant and powerful silence, but they couldn't soothe me. My apartment was as empty as my heart. My wife had left me because I had given all of it to my job, and even when I did spend time with her, my mind was still at work. She had lost hope, and I couldn't blame her. I tried to handle the situation the same way I usually handled my challenges at work, believing that for every problem, there is a solution, but this time there wasn't. We had an amicable divorce, but now all I had left was work and my close family. I had no friends.

"Can you come in after tomorrow? We have a new assignment starting." My boss knew I had five vacation days scheduled, but he asked anyway because it's always "customer first" at McKinsey, and I couldn't say no. The deep silence that couldn't soothe me had grown, evolving into a heaviness that never left. I couldn't help wondering what had gone wrong. I was successful and having fun, so why did I feel so bad? Why did I feel too weak just to say no for once? I loathed myself for this, and the feeling became unbearable. Two days later, I was bombarded with information in my new client's meeting room, but it went in one ear and out the other. I couldn't retain anything, and at night I couldn't sleep. How had I gotten there?

Three days later, I went to see my boss: "My divorce is catching up with me. I can't concentrate."

"You have a year," he said. "Come back whenever you want."

I don't know which was the greater revelation – the relief that flooded me or the realization that all along I had only needed to ask.

There is no such thing as chance... but maybe opportunities arise for us to better balance our professional, private, and personal lives.

It was raining outside. Old advertising posters clung to the walls. The furniture in this place had last been in fashion several years ago, probably at the tail-end of this company's glory years. These are just details, but you tend to notice them when you're a roving management consultant.

Inside I met Margie, a woman in her early thirties, smartly dressed, energetic, and blessed with a gentle smile. She welcomed me into her office, where reports were neatly filed on the shelves behind her desk, a desk on which a computer, a notebook, and three folders lay perfectly arranged. She invited me to sit at her conference table. It was a little big for this room, so I squeezed between it and the wall. Calculations and detailed diagrams filled the whiteboard behind my back. "Can I get you a glass of water?" she began.

Margie was the daughter of an industry captain. Her father ran an international conglomerate employing over 35,000 people. With experience as an investment banker and a venture capitalist, she had returned two years earlier to take on operational responsibilities at the firm. She reported to Henry, an accountant who became chairman of the group's most prominent business unit. He had the soul of a true competitor. An excellent sportsman, he loved to challenge those closest to him. He was demanding, protective, and surrounded by a team of loyal seconds who appreciated his perfectionist approach.

Henry had a natural affinity with structures and processes. He excelled at organizing and planning operational activities. Consequently, this company's processes were all clearly defined, and each employee was trained, monitored, evaluated, and coached. The annual chairman's awards recognized and rewarded the best teams, and any unprofessional behavior or declines in performance were recorded and communicated openly.

Naturally, everyone working there lived in constant fear of being publicly shamed. Those winning under this regime were confident stars with a tendency to look down on others, and if they knew any best practices that could've helped a colleague, they knew better than to share them because that might lose them their elite status.

So Margie found herself working in what felt like a Soviet-era surveillance state where neighbors betrayed neighbors. When she took the position, she inherited a history of poor results and a management team sitting firmly in its comfort zone. Latent conflicts smoldered between departments, and employee engagement was low. She felt that Henry had not taken adequate steps to improve the situation and that he was not supporting her. During board meetings, she was often blamed for the company's problems, but he never once spoke up in her defense.

"I'm fed up, and I've been thinking about returning to my old employer," she eventually told me. Feeling slightly squashed as I was between the table and the wallchart, I still felt a lot less constricted than Margie did because, for her, it wasn't just about the job. "My father doesn't see all the effort I am putting in. It's been like this forever. He always appreciated my brothers more than me."

There is no such thing as chance… but maybe circumstances sometimes invite us to revisit our emotional wounds and find our superpowers.

You might rightly ask: What is the link between these stories, and why does this sentence *"There is no such thing as chance…"* keep appearing?

I believe that we receive the experiences we unconsciously choose and that these challenges build us so they don't happen by chance. They are the consequences of momentous events in which we need to find ourselves, but we usually don't realize this until afterward. The further we go in life, the more we can "connect the dots," as Steve Jobs said.

Daniel, Margie, and I faced an unpleasant storm that pushed us to our limits. How we got into our individual states of turmoil was rooted in our personal stories, but these destabilizing events forced us all to change direction and go back to basics. They prompted us to make radical choices. They offered us powerful learning opportunities. They made us vulnerable and human. This is why I see them as valuable gifts.

A leader can falter but must quickly regain alignment to make the right decisions.

Storms come from many different sources: bad decisions, a misalignment of values, unexpected accidents, unmanaged work-life balance, limiting beliefs, personal emotional wounds, or well-meaning partners who unintentionally infect us with their own concerns.

My observation is that there is some driving force behind every storm, and yes, I'm saying that the difficulties we encounter don't happen by chance but by design. You might reasonably ask who I think is responsible for creating them, but I can't be sure. Is it us or some higher power? For me, it doesn't matter; the fact is that such things happen to us, and they push us to behave in specific ways that disrupt our equilibrium and help us to grow. Each of these events is a gift that can bring us face-to-face with the parts of us that need to evolve.

This is a law of nature, and we may only exist (both as individuals and as a species) because our ancestors faced such challenges, rose to meet them, and grew. Storms drive our personal evolutions and human evolution as a whole, but only if we choose to respond to these gifts. Becoming aware of our veiled drivers means understanding how we relate to ourselves and others. This is essential if we want to navigate the vulnerable, complex, uncertain, and ambiguous world we live in with serenity and strength.

Look Below The Surface

Don't believe it because it is said by an authority, angels, God, or an inspired source.

Believe only because you have explored it in your own heart, thoughts, and body and found your truth.

— Gautama Buddha

Do you know why firefighters, paramedics, and soldiers undergo so much training before being allowed to apply it in real-life situations? It's because when their jobs throw them into chaotic and frightening scenes, they must be able to respond with the correct behaviors quickly and decisively. People's lives are on the line, so they cannot afford to let their thoughts and emotions take over.

How can we train ourselves to respond quickly and decisively to all the new challenges that today's C-suite leaders may face? We can prepare with real-life case studies, of course, which are particularly useful, but how do we cope with the rapid onslaught of new challenges that Artificial Intelligence, Blockchain, Biotechnology, Drones, Solar Energy, Quantum Computing, Nanotechnology, 3D Printing, Self-driving Cars and Robots generates? How do we attract and retain talents? We know it's by having a definite purpose and sustainable values, but are they genuinely relevant in today's environment? How do we motivate Gen Z to go the extra mile and not just do the bare minimum? How do we face difficult conversations and challenges instead of quitting? How do we explain that effort is more satisfying in the long run than seeking instant gratification?

We can't look for solutions in the past, nor can we observe other players. We must still move forward despite the uncertainty, be confident that we are making the right decisions, be present with all our senses but not stressed, be persistent in our intentions but not rigid in our actions and be resilient in the face of the unexpected but not agitated. These capacities can't be found outside of ourselves. We must look inside, deep within our hearts and souls.

> *"Why are you here on earth, in this family, and doing this job?" asked Ben during an Executive retreat I was facilitating.*
> *"To earn money," answered Tim.*
> *"Yes, but why?" continued Ben.*
> *"To be the best in our markets."*
> *"Why?"*
> *"To best serve our clients and stakeholders."*
> *"Why?"*
> *"To provide a good life for my family."*
> *"Why?"*
> *"To be good… To do good… Yes, to do good!" When Tim repeated this, you could almost see the lightbulb switching on above his head. He had finally drilled down to the truth about what motivated him.*

After college, Tim joined his brother Chris in their newly launched vegetable production business. The work was hard. The employees came from simple backgrounds. The company had to compete against well-established players, but Chris and Tim were ambitious and unafraid. Their father had taught them some great values:

> *"To succeed, always be humble and join forces with someone better than you."*

In thirty years of hard work, they had built an empire. Many of the original employees were still with them and were now in positions of responsibility. The group had diversified. The start-up had become a listed company and had partnered with world leaders.

But when COVID arrived, Chris buckled and left. Tim was abroad when this monster storm hit the family and staff. Tim had to take charge of the group quickly. "I'm here to do good," he recalls saying. COVID restrictions put tremendous pressure on operations. Sales were collapsing, banks were getting restless, and the staff feared for their health and livelihoods. Chris's departure had left an enormous void, and Tim had to act wisely. "I am here to do good" was the mantra he shared with everybody. But what did "do good" mean for him, his family, his board, his employees, the banks, and his clients? "Good" could mean something different to all of them, so which "good" should he be chasing?

When Tim came to me for help, we identified five guiding principles that became his list of reference points for making important decisions, his checklist to explain what "do good" meant at every crossroads. Two years later, no employees had been fired, all activities were profitable, and the group had several million in cash to invest in new projects.

Like at sea, the storm lashes the surface, but everything beneath is peace and serenity. The same should be true of you.

I am passionate about understanding human behaviors and have come across many tools that help me clarify what drives them. During my university years, I was particularly interested in Carl Gustav Jung. I felt an affinity with his thoughts, and his personality theory made sense. After discovering the MBTI, Insights, DISC, and other personality tests, I was quickly hooked, but I still felt that these tools were missing something. Indeed, there was more to the human personality than the descriptions they offered.

During my first business appraisals, I discovered the competency models that every sound performance management system uses. Although very useful for HR professionals, they are complex tools to apply. Moreover, they do not work with fascinating but atypical people. The war for talent reinforced the need to attract and retain such people.

They wanted to work for companies with solid values that they could identify with, so leaders began defining them and have been doing so ever since.

Corporate values are important because they give work another layer of meaning. However, the more I accompany elite executives, the more I realize that something profound is still missing. The books of Dale Carnegie, Peter Drucker, Tom Peters, Stephen Covey, Daniel Goleman, Jim Collins, Fred Kofman, and Jon Kabat-Zinn are long-standing best-sellers. Emotional intelligence, Authentic Communication, and Mindfulness are taught in training centers worldwide. Still, while this is all helpful, none of it explains some of the strange behaviors I observe with many unique talents.

I started thinking about this after Margie had listened to my advice and asked me: "Do you have anything else?" I didn't, which is how she became the catalyst for my dive into a subject I had long feared to approach. It was time to look into the paranormal and subtle forces for explanations. I explored esoteric ideas such as energy psychology, shamanic medicine, and quantum philosophy, all surprisingly accessible topics. They offer solutions for transgenerational links and field-related interactions. Becoming a practitioner of ancestral processes, I learned to be transparent and let the universal energy do its work. I confess that I have difficulty explaining what is happening when I engage in these practices as it destabilizes my rational and controlling mind, but it works.

In putting all these tools together, I realized that two states of mind trigger all the other forces and make us walk on different paths. Either we are driven to survive and protect our assets, or we are driven to evolve into abundance and the unknown.

THE PATHS

Survive or Die

The Big History Project tells us that our solar system began to form around four billion years ago. Still, the figure might as well be fourteen billion (the supposed age of the universe) because I can't fathom the vastness of that much time from the perspective of my brief little life.

The first homo sapiens arrived 350,000 years ago, or 0.00875% of the earth's lifetime—another number that seems too elusive to appreciate fully. We formed our first significant agricultural communities and cities only 5,000 years ago, which is much easier to get a sense of. If a generation comes along every twenty five years, that's 200 births ago when we first began to regulate human behavior by organizing people into communities. As these early settlements grew, direct verbal communication was no longer enough to guarantee order. The most crucial information had to be written down.

Surprisingly, writing began with the need for accurate accounting. The amount of grain produced or water consumed had to be monitored, so even at the dawn of history, CFOs already had their fingers on the pulse. It was only a brief time before our human communities were regulating themselves and, eventually, almost every other species on the planet.

What do we have that makes us this powerful? Some will say it's our adaptability, but what does that mean? Others will point to our intelligence and rationality. They have certainly helped, but we're driven by something more profound, ancestral, and primitive than that. We are just incredibly good at surviving. Let's see how that works…

Today there are eight billion people on earth. When I was born in the 1950s, there were only two billion of us, and in 1900, when my grandfather was born, the world population was only one billion. Our species grew eight times within three generations!

Imagine owning hundred square meters (about 1,100 square feet) of land. On the surface, you might find flowers, grass, butterflies, bees, birds, spiders, mice, and more. Still, the soil beneath will teem with millions of other organisms, including earthworms, slugs, larvae, mites, and animals too small for the naked eye to see, like protozoa and nematodes, all of them working in perfect equilibrium with each other. But equilibrium doesn't mean static because the balance between these creatures and their environment is constantly in flux, pushing and pulling, rising and falling.

Now let's imagine that the mouse population on this patch of land multiplies by eight times in just a few months. How will this affect their 'world'? They will likely be hyper-stressed, hungry, and tense from a lack of food and living space. Being in a permanent state of alert will weaken their immune systems. Diseases will spread quickly and wipe out the weakest, but in time, nature will correct the population explosion and restore homeostasis. The most agile and resilient creatures survive and evolve to enjoy the next state of harmony, and this lasts until the next great storm arrives to disrupt it.

The SARS, MERS, Ebola, Zika, H1N1, and COVID epidemics of the last twenty years followed these rules, and so did the financial crises that arose simultaneously. There was the internet bubble of 2000 (where I lost sixty percent of my liquidity), the 2008 subprime crash (where I lost twenty five percent of my remaining assets), and the great resignation stimulated by the 2020 lockdowns.

If we were just an animal like mice, we humans would have been "regulated" a long time ago. So, what else have we developed that makes us survive?

Body, Mind, and Something Else

One of my early teachers said: "Our brains evolved into three areas. The first is found in all reptilians and manages biological processes. The second, the limbic brain, is where our emotions begin, and the third, the cortex, is responsible for perception and cognition."

I like the simplicity of this model. It casts us as a physical body governed by a reptilian brain that uses our instinctual intelligence to ensure our immediate physical survival, and a treasure trove of emotions built from our past experiences and stored in our limbic brain regulates our social relationships. It is a world of abstract thoughts that analyze the past and imagine the future to help us make the right decisions now.

All these capacities serve five vital needs. They help us:

1. to feed ourselves
2. to procreate and ensure the survival of our species
3. to dominate others and thus better serve the first two needs
4. to conserve energy, so we are ready to deal with imminent danger or food scarcity
5. to quickly recognize danger and respond

Unfortunately, there is a catch to this system. It doesn't work well when our survival needs are met. Without opposing forces, we become addicted to dopamine discharges. Our emotions and thoughts become unstoppable and destructive, which helps to explain these observations:

1. Eating disorders such as bulimia or anorexia have increased rapidly over the last few decades.
2. Pornography accounts for thirty percent of all web traffic.
3. Shopping for luxury products and the race for views on social networks are becoming priorities for communities with stable incomes.
4. Modern gadgets are seducing us into neglecting our minds and bodies.
5. We are saturated with media that bombard us with useless but attention-grabbing information.

"Is it all that simple? Are we just a body with some emotions and thoughts inside?" asked the young girl sitting close to me on the train. She had been reading my notes as I wrote. "What else could it be?" I asked. "The Little Prince," she answered proudly with a smile.

What an amazing, not to mention clairvoyant little girl! Yes, there is something more to us; it goes by many names: wisdom, inspiration, intuition, presence, consciousness, essence, source, spirit, or "The Little Prince." In the book, the Little Prince teaches us to look beneath the surface to find the true meaning of things. He shows us that by acting responsibly in our relationships with others, we gain a greater understanding and appreciation of our responsibilities to the broader world. Maybe I should read this brilliant book one more time.

While talking with the little girl, her brother played in the aisle, swinging between two rows of seats. Caught up in his imaginary game, he sang louder and louder. "That's enough now. Can't we have some peace on this train? This child has no manners," said a loud voice. The kid stopped. Surprised and frightened, he ran to sit next to his mother, who was dozing. "Why are people angry?" the little girl asked me. Young children ask the most important questions!

When danger threatens us, our famous **fight or flight** reaction still takes over, but it should be called the **fight, flight, or freeze response** because playing dead is something else that evolution has ingrained in us.

These three survival responses are still embedded within us, but they haven't helped us achieve dominance of the earth. That's more to do with our intelligence, not necessarily as individuals, but as the ultimate pack animals. Very early in our evolution, we understood that we were safer and more robust in groups, which led our limbic or emotional brain to make a quantum leap in development.

The Four Human Qualities

René Descartes, the French philosopher, believed the human pineal gland to be the "principal seat of the soul." Hence, it seems appropriate to place consciousness in the center of the following diagram to illustrate the four human qualities.

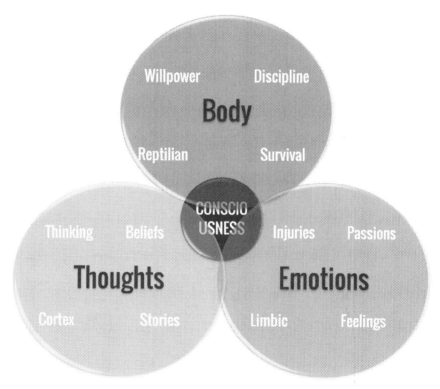

CHART 1: The Four Human Qualities

The first quality is the awareness of our physical body. This is where we satisfy our vital needs. It is here that we develop courage, willpower, and discipline. We look for many ways to become "fitter," so we spend much time and money on things like diets, exercise, and supplements.

The second quality is the awareness of our thoughts. It is the place of our beliefs and imagination and the source of our judgments.

The third quality is the awareness of our emotions. Emotional intelligence has been offered in management training for the past two decades. This is where we "feel" the information we gather. This receptacle of our past pleasant and unpleasant experiences forms the content of our emotions and desires and is the source of our suffering.

The fourth quality is the awareness of our consciousness or "presence," a field of study that is gradually gaining attention from the business community. Mindfulness training and quantum science can validate or challenge old religious beliefs, and it's here in the realm of soul consciousness that we can connect with something greater than ourselves. It is a state of being where we feel detached and free from suffering, identity, and judgment.

The others hide the fourth quality in this diagram because this is how we usually function. We tend to let everyday physical sensations, emotions, and thoughts obscure our soul consciousness. Still, we often become aware of this pure intelligence when situations like a spiritual quest or an extremely difficult experience raise it to the surface. In this book, I intend to help you access this fantastic quality whenever you want.

Our Friend Ego

I don't know about you, but I constantly oscillate between "good" and "evil." On the one hand, I regulate myself and others to ensure fairness for all. On the other hand, I look for loopholes in the system to gain personal advantage. Let's look deeper at the ego and its bad reputation.

"I should get rid of my ego" is a phrase I often hear but disagree with. Without it, we would not be here. It's a friend who constantly serves us, especially when storms arrive. It makes us vigilant in the face of danger, seeking allies and making judgments. It alerts us to threatening situations and guides our responses, but in the absence of real threats, it can become our enemy.

Our bodies, emotions, and thoughts are on alert when danger threatens us. They manifest themselves so intensely that consciousness and presence take a back seat. Our ego takes over. Pain avoidance and pleasure-seeking become our primary drivers. It gives us the energy to find safety at all costs. Once there, if we continue to pursue sensual rewards, we disconnect ourselves from more profound wisdom and want to stay in our conform zone. We act without moderation. We seek to possess the things we desire. We become transactional and materialistic. The fear of dying, losing money, becoming dependent on others, aging, or falling ill may all possess us.

Our true self knows that we need a certain amount of suffering to evolve. Without hunger, we cannot fully appreciate the food offered to us. Without war, we cannot enjoy peace. Only after we experience particularly unpleasant moments can we truly savor the wonder of the present moment. The path to the true north does not lie in complacency and comfort. It is found by examining in detail the nature of our unpleasant emotions, limiting beliefs, and painful feelings. When I observe, understand, and embrace my suffering, I allow compassion and love to grow in me and around me.

Why is it so difficult to escape from our pleasure-seeking and discomfort-avoiding side? Let's imagine that we need to cross a field that's packed with dense vegetation. The first thing we need to do is clear a path with machetes. Once we have created this small trail, it's the only one we'll take. We never make another, and soon it becomes well-worn.

The same principle applies to the synaptic paths we create during the first months after birth. Each time a similar sensation, emotion, or thought is re-experienced, our system will follow the same mental pathway we cleared with our first experiences. These neural networks are myelinated. Myelin is a substance that surrounds the neurons so that they conduct electricity. This substance is abundant before the age of eight and during puberty, which is why our childhood patterns of thoughts and behaviors persist throughout our lives. They become hardwired, and forever after, these pathways act like filters that make us see life subjectively.

A baby elephant can be punished into accepting a solid chain on its foot and no longer trying to escape so that by the time it's an adult; its handlers only need to use a rope to enforce its ongoing captivity. Similarly, what we experience and how others react to us helps us to quickly understand which behaviors and experiences are rewarding and which are not. If mom feeds us at the first sign of hunger, our approach to the relationship will be calm and constructive, and we will feel confident. But if we are not satisfied immediately, fear stimulates us to start waving our little arms around. If food appears, we now understand that we must be active to get what we want.

If the food still doesn't come, we cry and scream, and if it does arrive at this point, we now understand that this is what it takes to get what we need. A tantrum equals a reward. But if the food still doesn't come, we will eventually be forced to shut up and wait. We become submissive. Suppressing our emotions and freezing when in danger are our only strategies. The more we experience events like these, the more our reactional behaviors become anchored.

Depending on which approach worked best for us, we will continue to use the mental pathway we first cleared with our metaphorical machete and reinforce it during our first encounters with strangers, especially in kindergarten and beyond.

The kids conditioned into silence early on will observe the dance between bully and victim and avoid conflicts. Later, as grown-ups at work, where disputes are more diffuse and subtle, they will want to ignore or dodge these situations. Having gotten what they wanted through yelling and hitting, other children will feel comfortable with conflict and will not hesitate to pressure others.

We may go through our entire lives not appreciating how conditioned we are and how much that conditioning affects our behavior. I suggest stepping back and making a conscious decision to examine your inner narrative. Here's mine, taken to its extreme:

I care about myself first and foremost. As an alpha male, I feel superior. I identify with those who are similar. I gain strength from those who live and think like me. I know we are right. Those who are different make me angry. I constantly observe and judge what they do. I am very conscious of my appearance and take pride in it. I dominate others with arrogance and indifference. When things don't happen as they should, it's their fault. There is no question about it. I confidently ride the wave of success until the s*** hits the fan. An illness, a mistake, a promotion I don't get, a failure I have to accept. Any unwelcome surprise like this derails me. A storm has arrived. I feel lost and vulnerable.

I need to hide. A depressive mood overtakes me. I ruminate on the same issues over and over. I envy those who seem more successful and look for the weaknesses or privileges they might have. Soon, thoughts about the future and the past will haunt me. I struggle to accept the uncertainty of my current situation. I become very possessive and fearful of losing everything. I flee into illusory hopes and dreams. When I look back over my past, regrets come. I feel guilty for my abusive actions and sad that I didn't do what was right. The weight on my shoulders grows. I have little energy left to fight. I take refuge in addictions such as coffee, nicotine, food, work, flirting, alcohol, pills, and even drugs, and it becomes a vicious circle. An enormous storm is arriving. "There is no such thing as chance..." comes to my mind, "But I don't want this chance," my ego answers.

Of course, this can start off feeling uncomfortable. Still, if you take a step back and consciously follow the route your thoughts naturally take, you will uncover inbuilt tendencies that you may not have been aware of. The paths you laid down in childhood may be well-worn, but as an adult, you can recognize them, and then take others.

The chart below helps us understand the different emotions we experience in the ego or **survival state**. We first look at ourselves, and depending on our level of self-confidence, we might feel superior or inferior. When we feel self-assured and arrogant, others will trigger our anger if they don't do what we expect from them. When we feel insecure and depressed, we will envy others and complain. In any case, we will separate from all those who differ from us and judge them to justify our choice.

Our thoughts are very much conditioned by our future and our past. We hope for better times or fear losing our current advantages and routines. Looking at the past, we may feel sadness, guilt, shame, and disgust depending on our capacity to deal with our suffering.

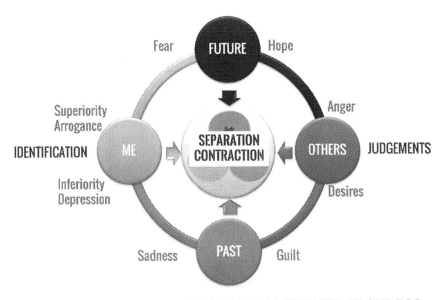

CHART 2: EMOTIONAL REACTION WHEN ACTIVATED BY OUR EGO

We all perceive the world differently, according to our own experiences, beliefs, education, and previous encounters. As I said, our mental constructs are acquired early in childhood and stay with us. If we remain asleep to our conditioning, then we may not be so well prepared when the storms inevitably come.

We, humans, have faced frequent environmental changes throughout our evolution, and there are more on the way today. One of my firm beliefs about nature is its constant aim to compensate for the imbalances generated by external and internal pressures and to restore an ideal

MARC-ANTOINE TSCHOPP

equilibrium between all beings and their environment. I've noticed that when I see a possible solution to correct momentary imbalances with my resources, I perceive the situation as a positive challenge, and my energy level rises. But when I feel trapped without the choice to change something, the challenge becomes unpleasant, and my energy diminishes. So, it is not the challenge that creates stress but my reaction to it. Here comes my friend ego again. I can let it react or choose to act more consciously. It's true, though, that there are limits. The more simultaneous threats I must deal with, the more stretched I feel, and the less I can adapt.

Stress is an adaptive survival reaction. It is a reorganization of our energy capacities to adapt to pressure changes. It is a beneficial reaction that allows us to face a new situation. Its intensity depends on two factors.

The first is a change in the level of external, objective stressors. Examples include financial difficulties, health problems, death, moving house, unrealistic deadlines, conflicting relationships, contradictory orders, urgency, unexpected demands, complexity, stubborn bureaucracy, audits, etc.

The other factor is what I call 'stressability.' This is our subjective interpretation of challenges according to our physical, emotional, and mental state. It is this factor that causes the most problems.

You have probably heard or read that we need to manage our stress by using relaxation techniques or reorganizing our lives to alleviate the pressures that affect us. This is partially true and requires further analysis. One study analyzed the mortality rates of 30,000 American experiencing stress over eight years. The results were surprising. People with low-stress and high-stress lives had nearly identical mortality rates when the high-stress group didn't think their stress was harming them. But a third subgroup of highly stressed people who believed their stress was bad for them had a forty three percent higher risk of dying.

So, our stressability or attitude toward stress matters the most. If we think stress is negative, it will be harmful. But seeing it as an energy to be used consciously can make us more intelligent, confident, and empathetic. "*Stress can even improve our health. The best way to deal with stress is not to fight it but to welcome it. You can't anticipate it.*

It is a sudden phenomenon that occurs only in the present and tells us something important about a current event. Constant anticipation of challenges reinforces our feeling of being able to control everything. When the unexpected happens, we feel powerless, which amplifies the stress," explains Professor Kelly McGonigal, a health psychologist, and lecturer at Stanford University.

Although we are not all equal when it comes to stress, because serotonin levels differ from one individual to another, we can all train ourselves to improve our stressability. There are many ways of doing so, and this book is one of them; so, keep reading! In the meantime, you can measure your stressors and stressability by clicking the following link:

https://www.podnow.org/solutions/gestion-du-stress/

My parents used to get one to three letters in their mailbox weekly and had a siesta every day after lunch. Today many of us feel bad if we haven't responded to a hundred texts and emails before we start work. Some people spend all day running from meeting to meeting and finally begin the real work when everybody has left the office, and for those working from home, it can be even worse. Some must wait until everybody is asleep before getting any quality work done. So many people are hyperactive, in a frantic rush to do things while rarely questioning their usefulness or importance. They wait for weekends and vacations to stop this frenzy, and when the downtime finally arrives, and they allow themselves to relax, they get sick. Some can't even do that, and burnout carries them to the hospital.

A few years back, when the French Ministry of Health surveyed the world of work, it found some alarming results: fifty six percent of employees were unable to concentrate because they had to react to unforeseen and urgent requests, thirty three percent said they received contradictory instructions and had no room to maneuver or no real responsibility, thirty three percent suffered from conflict with their superiors, colleagues or clients, twenty five percent found that planned deadlines were impossible to meet, and twenty four percent said they felt abandoned by their leaders.

As leaders, especially of the younger generations, we must face these critical challenges. How do we keep people busy and engaged, so they can effectively manage the storms that lie ahead without pushing them into hyperactivity? How do we convey a sense of hope in the future when so much is in decline? How can we inspire people to trust us when they are the ones who must fix our generation's mistakes? It's only by being very clear about our **true north**, by behaving genuinely, and by communicating powerfully that we can hope to succeed. It's like riding a wave. We can't do it in theory. We must feel it for ourselves and practice all the moves until we've nailed it.

When There is Not Enough

Claude was considered the warehouse unionist. Courageous and strong-minded, he often gathered his colleagues in the locker room to share his opinions on the reorganizations imposed by their boss. We were upgrading our computer system, and the teams had to be open to the critical changes to come. I had sympathy for Claude. I never saw him complain for his own sake. It was always for the good of his colleagues. He reminded me of my savior side. One morning, I passed him in the workshop. He was cutting electric cables by hand, which are heavy and difficult to handle. He was precise, fast, and meticulous, and as I watched him, an idea came to me. "I have a deal for you. You teach me your job, and I'll teach you mine. We'll do this for one day, okay?" He stopped and thought it over, before saying with a sly smile, "Okay."

The next day, I was sweating as I struggled to cut thick cables with those little scissors. It all felt so unfamiliar and I'm sure he could tell I was out of my depth. "This is not an easy job. Now I understand why you're always asking for better tools," I said.

The following day it was his turn in my shoes. He sat in my big, comfortable CEO chair, and I handed him a folder from my in-tray. "You need to read this and decide what we should do." He looked as panicked as I had with the scissors in my hand. He started to read. "But how do you decide?" he answered. I explained my reasoning for the first one then handed him a second folder. "This is what you do all day?," he said. "I wouldn't sleep at night with all these questions in my head. I don't know how you do it."

Since then, we have become friends. The operational reorganization proposals were discussed without any ulterior motives. The labels of unionist and boss had lost their shine.

A belief is a very personal, constructed thought. We are convinced that our beliefs are valid, accurate, and authentic. A combination of opinions expressed in our childhood and reinforced by our past experiences will form a paradigm. This very subjective worldview serves as a reference point in our daily actions. It becomes the basis for our judgments about ourselves, others, or even the weather, and our prejudices reinforce them. They allow us to believe that the world is how we want to see it, so we can never be wrong. This comes in handy when battling storms and our ego is on high alert. Our prejudices keep us safe…right up to the moment when reality destroys those cherished beliefs.

We are all familiar with this process. We only need to remember our adolescence and its illusions. I like how David Whyte, an Irish poet, has summarized them. We start by believing that, as an individual, we are immune to any physical, financial, or emotional difficulties. In relationships, we are sure we will never have our hearts broken, not by our partners, children, friends, or passions. Finally, we are confident we can easily plan and organize our future to ensure we achieve our first two illusions. Life starts straightforward and stays that way until a good, solid storm throws us out of our comfort zone.

I have noticed how talented young adults will now leave companies they find too restricting, how they are less keen to invest in non-sustainable goods and services, and how they connect more with nature and pursue healthy activities and hold values that are often incompatible with traditional educational and professional cultures. It is clear to me that our dominant paradigms need to be revisited. They challenge the notion that our economies can continue their present trajectories forever, and they have a point. Our planet has finite space and resources, so we either reduce the number of people on it or create a two-tier world. At the top, the wealthy will protect their assets by whatever means they can, while at the bottom, everyone else will need to be paid, entertained, and monitored closely to avoid unrest.

Such a grim world will put us all on permanent high alert, so we, or rather you, as a fully conscious leader, must either focus on avoiding such dystopias or making them more livable.

Grow in the Unknown

A dream came true. I was very excited as I put my suit on and surprised because I thought it would be heavier. An instructor repeated a lesson we had heard many times already because those guys live and breathe safety. This was serious now. I walked across the tarmac proudly, helmet on, towards the pink Pilatus waiting with its doors wide open. Four experienced jumpers welcomed us. I chose mine and the plane took off. We were hiding our fear by joking and laughing, but at four thousand meters, my buddy opened the door and hiding wasn't an option anymore. I sat before him while he attached my straps to his parachute. Fear gripped me. I stiffened and looked at my partner. Was he experienced? Was I strapped in correctly? Would he fall on me when we landed? I must remember to bend my knees…

My ruminations stopped when he pushed me into the void. I was flying above the whole world and accepting it was my only choice. Fear turned to joy.

Fear of the unknown is a natural emotion that engages all our senses and memories of past experiences to evaluate new risks. Once we accept the challenge of the unknown, we enter a new reality. It is like diving into a lake for the first time without knowing how to swim. A wave of new sensations overwhelms us, but if we let go and welcome this new reality, a seductive learning experience will enliven our senses.

The weather was beautiful. My wife Patricia was delighted and proud. This Sunday was the first time in thirty years that all her brothers and sisters had gathered on the same continent. The party was joyful, and the siblings had a deep sense of connection. Jo, Patricia's twenty-nine-year-old niece, arrived at the last minute. She was like a third child to Patricia, and Jo now thought of me as her second father after her dad's death three years earlier.

The whole family went on an excursion the next day, but Jo decided to stay with us. She wanted to do a photo shoot and arranged a makeup artist and photographer for the following day. While chatting she revealed that her mother was depressed, and her brother was lost in fantasies. She assumed responsibility for the family when her father left after feeling guilty for leaving home at nineteen. "You left me alone," he had told her on his deathbed.

The phone rang the next day at 5:30 am. It was the makeup artist. Jo was not answering her calls. Patricia went to her room and found Jo lying dead in the shower. A part had broken off in the boiler, and she had been electrocuted.

The long-awaited joy turned to tremendous pain in a matter of seconds. A mother had lost another family member. A disconnected brother now faced an unbearable reality. Adoptive parents were experiencing sadness, anger, and guilt. It took time for them to heal but eventually, everyone gained something of value from this tragedy. Patricia became more aware of life's fragility and impermanence and her yoga teaching became more sincere and assertive. The journey was long for the mother and brother and included quitting addictive behaviors. For other family members, their bonds have strengthened and continue to grow.

The five stages of grief are denial, anger, bargaining, depression, and acceptance, and anyone losing a child may linger in the pain of the first four for a long time. The dictionary may define suffering as pain, but I prefer to consider it the gap between what is true and what we would like our reality to be. The greater the gap, the more we suffer. I'm not suggesting that physical and emotional agony aren't real, but I am saying that our attitude toward them can profoundly reduce how much they hurt us. The stoics knew this in ancient Greece, and their ideas can still be found in cognitive and behavioral therapy today.

But reducing pain alone doesn't guarantee happiness. To do that, we need to ensure that the things we spend most of our time doing are the ones that make us happy. It's a state of engagement first described by Professor Mihaly Csikszentmihalyi in his **flow** theory. In the early 1990s, he found that everyone had so-called "optimal experiences." In these moments, people had a strong sense of self-esteem. The vision of the goal they were trying to achieve was clear. As soon as something happened, they were immediately aware of it. They made decisions quickly and easily. When the situation became difficult, they persevered and learned from it, so they continued to develop. They let their creativity run wild and found practical solutions to their problems. Getting results was not their primary concern. They could work for a long time without feeling tired. The activity motivated them, and they experienced deep pleasure while working on it. They were in the flow of life.

In school, university, and our early working lives, we try different things, learn new skills and keep moving on to new challenges. Each one may give us some anxiety, but hopefully, we recognize that short-term pain is rewarded with long-term gain. Each new skill is a building block; we build on it even if it becomes outdated. We add to it. We suffer a little but keep on evolving. By persevering with each new activity, we quickly gain skills, so our excitement and commitment increase.

Eventually, we will become comfortable, routinely working in the flow and enjoying total control of our tasks. But without change, we will get bored again. Change means starting over, taking on a new, more demanding challenge, feeling anxious for a while as we strive to adapt, then getting in the flow once more. Throughout our lives, we will face these stages. If our stakes become too low, we regress into disempowerment and indifference. We then look for other sources of fulfillment. If not at work, then at home, in recreation, or community service.

Even as a ten-year-old, my friend Patrice chased the flow state. Money was the way to prove that he was superior to others. He loved making his classmates' coins disappear with dubious magic tricks (the money remains missing to this day). In his early twenties, he quit college to sell advertising space in telephone directories. He got into computers when they were new and traveled the world because he was convinced they would change it. Looking for more returns, he sold his company and went into real estate, modern arts, and vintage cars. He became totally engrossed in each new pursuit, finding his flow state each time, followed by a period of complacency, then boredom. His never-ending quest for money eventually became his nightmare. Convinced that profiteers surrounded him, he wanted to control everything and constantly fought with the IRS. His self-destructive addiction isolated him, and he was eventually caught out by a tax auditor and put in a mental health and addiction treatment center.

So, more than the search for flow alone is needed. We need to have a conscious purpose too. I have learned that every trial is a gift that lets me discover something important about myself. Whenever I suffer, I calm down and take the experience as an invitation. Admittedly, this is not always easy, especially when I'm pushed out of my comfort zone. And yet, this is precisely when creation, innovation, and learning occur. Connecting to what is happening now, without judging it, is the solution. Just be in the now, as Eckart Tolle said.

By calming our first three human qualities, body, emotions, and thoughts, our subtle presence can be fully expressed, allowing for more rewarding actions. By becoming more aware and open, we permit intuition to guide us. We develop the discipline to change our addictive habits. We become empathetic and genuinely compassionate with others. We make good, clear decisions. We confidently let go and allow the unknown to manifest freely. And most of all, we are agile, persistent, and resilient enough to follow our true north.

I call this attitude the **Mindset of Abundance**. It might seem similar to Carol Dweck's Growth Mindset, but I prefer the broader perspective that abundance suggests. We'll see that this matters when hard work and dedication are not enough to navigate us through unexpected storms. To explain this mindset, I created the following illustrations. At the center, we are animated by our consciousness. From this space, we look again at the world, but in an entirely different way than when our ego triggers us.

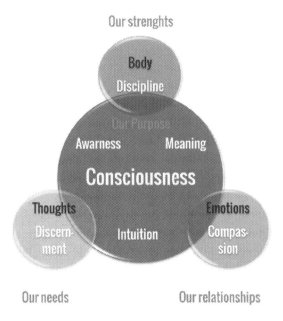

Our strenghts

Body
Discipline

Our Purpose

Awarness   Meaning

Consciousness

Thoughts   Emotions

Discern-   Intuition   Compas-
ment   sion

Our needs   Our relationships

CHART 3: FOUR HUMAN QUALITIES OF ABUNDANCE

Our four human qualities manifest themselves differently. We take a disciplined approach to keeping our bodies healthy. We welcome our emotions and leave room for genuine compassion in all our relationships. Our thoughts are fluid and precise, allowing us to make good decisions. We listen to our intuition and ensure that our actions align with our purpose and values.

More importantly, we don't need to learn new skills. The following chart shows that our world becomes abundant when our consciousness activates us. Our serenity, joy, and benevolence are undisturbed by the kind of phenomena that would generally unbalance us. Humility and understanding synchronicity (where significant and seemingly unconnected events co-occur) come naturally to us. It becomes easy to empathize with others and be non-judgmental. We can let go of unattainable goals and accept disturbances without fear. We free ourselves from past difficulties and are grateful for all the gifts we have received. Focusing on the present comes quickly and at will. Abundance is everywhere.

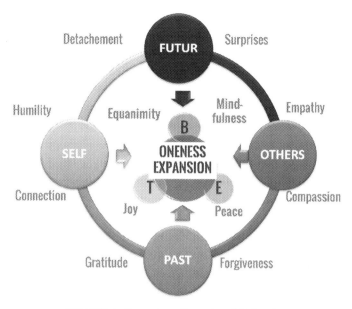

CHART 4: Conscious Emotional Behaviors

To find happiness, we must align with our true north. Only by looking honestly at ourselves can we define our **true north.**

Once You Achieve Money and Fame

"What do you need to be happy?" asked my father many years ago. I answered that question the same way most young people do: "money and fame."

I was forty one and married with two beautiful, healthy children when I decided to sell the family business and free myself from all the pressures a CEO must shoulder. With the time and money, this gave me I was finally free to live for my family and myself. I could finally be happy!

That was the theory, but I quickly tired of indulging myself. I wasn't just unhappy, I was also drifting into depression, but this was a gift because it taught me that I didn't have everything I needed. I could see that something important was missing and searching to find out what "happy" meant took me back to my first love, psychology. At this time in the US, the positive psychology movement was starting, and my research into it was exactly what I had been looking for. It reminded me of the interviews I conducted at McKinsey, finding what gave people the strength to persevere and succeed. AI had a different meaning then. It stood for Appreciative Inquiry, an organizational development model defined by David Cooperrider.

My quest for meaning and happiness grew in scope and intensity, and over the next twenty years, I followed many spiritual masters from every continent and background. They all taught me that life is a path, and at some point, they had all connected to the infinite life force with every cell of their being and systematically removed the emotional shackles that so often tie us down.

The more of these masters I met, the more I could see the distinction between those who explain and theorize and those who embody the life force in each of us through their pure actions and by speaking the truth. I understand that the latter has "simply" succeeded in transforming all the limitations we impose on ourselves. They live with simple compassion for all beings in our universe. They constantly connect with nature and express gratitude for every little thing that life offers them. They all arrived at this state of abundance via different paths. Each one took their own way but still found the exact endpoint of enlightenment, which means we can do the same!

My journey started very early in childhood when I deliberately tore my jeans to give them a unique look and let my hair grow, so I resembled one of the Beatles. As an adult, I stopped chasing fun and joined the social hierarchy. The many trials that followed allowed me to reconnect with myself and let go of certain beliefs. I went through a lot, but little by little, I found my true north. I have tried to codify what I have learned into the six steps for leadership in the storm, which I will share in the following chapters.

There is no one-size-fits-all solution for living. Using trial and error, we must define ourselves without regard for what other people think of us. I discovered that my reason for being is fulfilled **when the eyes of the people I meet shine**. I then established some guiding principles, and I've found that when I respect them, I feel more aligned with my true self. By trying to be as authentic and sincere as possible, I was able to test the strength of these principles and calmly face many uncertain and stressful situations. I synthesized them into a formula called "PODnow®." While I don't claim to have rid myself of all my conditioning, this formula helps me to move in that direction. After introducing it to thousands of people, I know it can help many more become happier and more effective. This book is the essence of my sixty-year quest. I am honored to share it with you.

How Much is Enough?

Matthew was a soon-to-be partner of one of the best consulting firms. As the son of a white Zimbabwean farmer who lost everything in early 2000, he knew he had no choice but to succeed. An ex-rugby player and father of two beautiful girls, he traveled the world with his wife, Elena. As a Swiss hotel management graduate, she knew how to support him fully. I saw sincere mutual admiration every time I met them. Matthew utilizes carbon revenues to restore natural forests and protect animals in his homeland. His commitment to the UN's Sustainable Development Goals helped him attract young talents worldwide. He regularly won prizes and gave talks about his venture. His positive attitude endeared him to all who had the chance to meet him.

Dhanesh wore a simple white robe and listened carefully when Matthew shared his fabulous story. That evening, as the three of us mulled over the day's events, Dhanesh noticed the beautiful Patek Philippe watch on Matthew's wrist. "What is it for?" he asked innocently.

"To keep track of the time," Matthew scoffed. "And how many of them do you have?" Dhanesh continued in his gentle voice.

"With this Nautilus, I have seven," and he went on to list a collection that could have bought a lovely house.

"And where are they?"

"In my safe, of course," he replied sharply.

Dhanesh told Matthew gently: "Mine cost less than ten dollars. It tells me the time, as well as yours, does. This watch is all I own. I have no value hiding anywhere else, and I am so happy. You will see, this too shall pass!" and with that, he left.

Matthew looked baffled. "What the f***?" he said. I then told him Dhanesh had been an Indian billionaire of the Jain religion. At seventy, he became a monk and gave away his entire fortune to his family and charity. He now walks barefoot, meditates a lot, and shares his wisdom when needed.

Matthew left later without saying goodbye. A few months later, I received a call: "Can you come? I'm lost. I feel like I've built my whole career out of filial duty. I don't know what I want anymore."

We become happiest in our work when we can apply our skills, when we receive sincere appreciation for our efforts, and when we have a worthwhile long-term goal. There is nothing wrong or selfish about being proud of our accomplishments. When we feel good about ourselves and what we do, we are more likely to share our skills with others and feel motivated to work harder and achieve more next time. We may even inspire others to achieve their own goals. Our confidence grows and allows us to seize each new opportunity with both hands.

But chaos will ensue when our work doesn't align with our happiness. Chasing money and fame is never-ending. The more we feed our ego, the bigger it grows and needs. It is a vicious circle that takes us further and further away from who we really are. We brag to reassure ourselves, surrounded by self-interested hangers-on who flatter us to our faces and sneer at us behind our backs. There are few people whom we can genuinely trust. We hide our vulnerability and protect ourselves from anything new. We strain to prove our worth in an exhausting race we can never win.

In the search for happiness, *"How much is enough?"* is a fundamental question that we can't answer without first asking, "Enough of what?" For that, we must look to ourselves and others to discover what we need, and how much of it will make us happy. When we know what we want, it becomes easier to abandon everything that doesn't align with our True North.

Trust Your Little Prince

"And now here is my secret, a very simple secret: It is only with the heart that one can see rightly; what is essential is invisible to the eye."

"Well, I must endure the presence of a few caterpillars if I wish to become acquainted with the butterflies."

—Antoine de Saint-Exupéry

Luigi was a doctor. He had worked with Professor Montagnier, the Nobel prize winner, and wanted to start a clinic for anticipatory medicine with me. I would take care of the mind. He would take care of the body. The business plan had to be ambitious. He had access to significant Qatari funding through a friend of the professor. We worked and dreamed for months. The crisis of 2008 had halved my coaching income, so I was looking forward to finally getting some funds. It was Christmas when Luigi called me: "It's okay, they agreed on ten million euros. The only problem is that they want to give it to the professor, who wants to use it for his projects." The axe had fallen, but my determination had not.

I convinced my wife that we should downsize to an apartment. I found a buyer, rented a place, hired employees, bought the machines, and invited the press to my opening. Fourteen months later, I closed the center and lost several hundred thousand euros. My potential customers had stayed away. My concept had been good, as several centers have been doing well using the same ideas ever since, but my approach at the time had yet to reach the target. I was guided by my ego and did not perceive the subtle signs of Life, nor did I listen to my inner wisdom. I knew my idea was right but I was impatient and rushed the execution.

My quest to learn from this led me to meet specialists on consciousness, neurospirituality, quantum mechanics, and altered states of consciousness. I will admit that the concepts are not always easy to accommodate, but I have found many ideas from these fields that work for me, so perhaps some of them might work for you too.

Saint-Exupéry's Little Prince speaks of a heart that sees what the eye cannot see. Today, transmission electron microscopy lets us see DNA, atoms, electrons, and protons. Everything at this miniature scale follows conventional physical laws. Still, beyond a certain point, you enter the realm of quantum mechanics, where a more powerful microscope would not help you make sense of it. At the level where we encounter photons, quarks, and other things that behave in bizarre ways, high school Newtonian physics breaks down. My point here is that although we may think we have a reality all figured out, we don't. Some weird laws in this universe don't care whether we believe in them. They exist anyway.

Einstein proved that space and time are not constant, and that matter and energy are interchangeable. Everything in the universe is constantly in motion, and it all vibrates at different frequencies. Light is a vibration, sound is a vibration, and even the solid-looking flesh of our bodies is composed of atoms—particles in constant motion that are mostly made up of empty space. The elements that make us were birthed in the death throes of exploding stars, so even the components of our physical selves have never stood still and never will. They all vibrate. We are composed of vibrations.

But if my body is a symphony of vibrations, then the 'me' that resides within it and looks out (the one that already knows all that I am sharing here) must be even more profound. I remember seeing a Kirlian photograph showing a glowing halo around fingers subjected to a high-frequency electrical field. This halo became known as an aura. As I researched this phenomenon further, I was pleased and surprised to discover that ancient philosophers, traditional healers, and women from all over the world have known about this subtle body of energy for a very long time. It is called the emotional, mental, astral, celestial, causal, etheric, energetic, or light body. It is interconnected with all the clusters of vibrations that surround it. If we accept the concepts of quantum mechanics, these clusters can occupy the same space simultaneously or remain connected across vast distances of space and even across generations.

Now I understand what the Little Prince meant when he revealed his secret, that our hearts can see the essentials better than our eyes.

If I want to perceive these fine forces, I must open my heart and mind to this new reality. In doing so, I can conceive what these scientists share: the knowledge that consciousness is not generated by the brain but exists outside it as a biofield. This explains why significant innovations, such as the steam engine, electricity, photography, telegraphy, and more were announced simultaneously on different continents before the internet, television, or radio appeared. This also explains why everyone in a room feels the energy of an angry or charismatic boss, even if they can't see them. Our environment influences everything we do. So, like Gandhi's famous sentence: "Be the change you want to see," if I want to access abundance, I should connect to kindness, happiness, and collaboration rather than anger, conflict, and separation. With this awareness, we understand that people and organizations are living systems and that the C-suite executive's purpose is to create well-being and prosperity for all so that all can flourish.

It may seem unrealistic to suggest that chief executives can become the engineers of workplace happiness when our management boards demand profits and our families require our love and commitment, but not only can these two worlds coexist peacefully, science has shown that they are complementary. Many studies have concluded that happy employees are more productive, engaged, agile, creative, and less stressed, which is good for them and the business.

What If There is Enough?

Paul stood alone at the sailing boat's bow, scanning the horizon. It had been two days since he had spoken to any of us. He was now waiting for just one thing—our return to port. He had been charming before, and we had all been contented. Everyone helped each other out and took turns with their tasks. We tucked the sails precisely and shared the cooking chores in a good-natured way. This atmosphere of cooperation made our hammocks seem more comfortable when we slept and the night shifts shorter when it was our turn to be awake, but then the depression came and threw us off course. We ended up much further north than we should have been and lost 3 to 4 days. We had no more fresh food, and even the toilet paper was gone. All that remained were cans, lots of cans. The holds were full of them, but we felt like we were running out. At night, alone on watch, I would gulp down a can of condensed milk and throw it overboard so no one else would know. They probably heard me, though, because I certainly heard them.

Have you noticed that we become more selfish when there is a shortage? As soon as we think we might run out of something, we panic and begin hoarding, as we did with toilet paper when the COVID lockdowns started. It only takes one media story to warn us of a shortage, which triggers us. The panic buying begins, even though we don't know whether the original story was true or not. That's how much we fear scarcity.

Some sources say that the earth's resources are dwindling and that soon there won't be enough for humans to live comfortably and peacefully. The media never fails to remind us that things are getting worse, but is it true? Some of the doom-laden prophecies are true. The human population has increased dramatically over the last century, with half of us now living in cities, with all of the problems that come with overcrowding. Biodiversity has decreased significantly, mainly due to man's irresponsible attitude, and the climate is changing to the point where humankind might not survive. It's all very worrying.

But before we fall into despair, let's look at some different information. Infant mortality has decreased by fifty percent in the last thirty years, illiteracy has fallen from sixty-eight percent to thirteen percent in just a century, the rate of malnourishment in the world decreased dramatically from twenty-five percent in 1990 to less than fifteen percent in 2017, the daily per capita caloric intake has increased by twenty-five percent globally in sixty years, only twenty-two percent of our agricultural land is devoted to crops, seventy percent of the earth's surface is water, and so far we have only discovered less than twenty percent of the animal kingdom.

If food is the issue, there is plenty of new solutions based on plant proteins (soy, peas), animal sources (insects), and biotechnological innovations (cultured meat or fungal proteins).

If water is the problem, improved drinking water technologies are being proposed by innovators from poor and rural backgrounds.

If air is the problem, just look at how quickly the skies of Delhi, Shanghai, and other big cities cleared during the COVID lockdowns.

If energy is the problem, look at how solar, wind, and wave power are evolving worldwide and how fusion now looks closer than ever.

The real problem has nothing to do with our physiological needs. It has to do with our mindset. We are facing evolution, a challenge that's a gift, an invitation to become more present, kind, loving, and aware. Once we accept that there is enough for everyone, we can appreciate and be grateful for all that life freely offers us. We understand that the true sign of progress is an open heart and education. We know that the quality of our relationships is the best measure of happiness. We feel that everything is interconnected. No one is better or worse than anyone else, and everyone is trying to do their best. We are simply different, and this diversity is our true wealth. We are free to search for our "true north" and our "compass" with serenity, knowing that we are already in the right place at the right time.

THE MAP

I hadn't seen her in six months. She had lost weight, her eyes looked dull and her shoulders were rounded. She smiled as we walked through the streets of Siracuse, telling me about her new life, her partner, and her plans, but her joy was fleeting. Everything Illona did was tell me that she was lost. This ray of sunshine who traveled the world giving yoga classes and sharing the art of healthy living, who set such an example to so many people, the one I love with all my heart, my daughter was lost, tired, and confused. I couldn't bear to see her like this. I had to help her. My questions became judgments.

"You look tired. I feel like you're letting yourself go. You have no energy. You need to take a break. You need to take care of yourself. You need to... You need to..."

"I know what to do, Dad. Thank you for your love, but I don't need you to tell me what to do," she replied, looking firm and fierce.

Thinking we know what's best for the people we love is a prime source of conflict, but the truth is that we don't know what's best for them any more than they know what's best for us. Our advice won't work despite our best intentions because everyone has to follow their own path to fulfillment. Perhaps that's why some saints lived in isolation in their caves. With no human interactions to disturb them, they could better connect with their true selves and pursue their quest for profound wisdom. But that's not what most of us can or want to do.

We usually are surrounded by people and animals with whom we interact permanently. If we care for them, we will be torn between taking care of ourselves and our relationships with others. As the following graph shows, we can represent these two opposing sets of needs as two axes on a graph to create a field that I call the "human relationship space." In this example, we have two individuals: me taking care of my happiness and someone else taking care of his. Both of us must take care of the relationship, but without being responsible for the other person's happiness! I know this may sound strange because we are taught to care for those we love, especially our children and those in need, but there are limits to what we should do. Let's talk about two responsible people who are both able to take care of themselves. Both are doing their best to respect each other as well as their relationship. Now let's see what happens when the ego steps in.

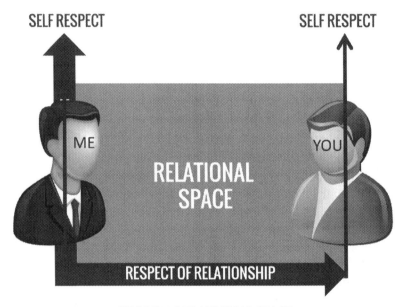

CHART 5: RELATIONAL SPACE

MARC-ANTOINE TSCHOPP

The Ten Survival Strategies

If you want to live in absolute hell, believe that you are responsible for what others feel.

—Marshall Rosenberg

As we already know, our friend ego is ready to step in and help us when storms arise. In this case, a storm threatens our relational space, and just like at sea, it makes waves. Our senses go on alert, and all our actions are directed at protecting us. Our sympathetic nervous system is activated. The heart rate increases, blood rushes to the muscles of the arms and legs, and the pupils and bronchial tubes dilate. The solar plexus becomes rigid, adrenaline and noradrenaline are secreted, and we experience fear, anger, and sadness. We react according to our usual neural programs. Some of us will flee, others will stay and fight, while others will silently endure the situation, hoping the storm will pass soon.

Many of today's businesses face big challenges as innovative attackers come at them from all sides. Large companies are taking advantage of storms in ways that others cannot and have become much more aggressive, while small companies are often really disruptive and creative. Financial instability and lack of employee engagement add to the pressure. Many C-suite executives feel threatened and react according to their state of mind. Some will want to leave, others will resort to authoritarian methods, and others will simply give up, focusing on protecting themselves from the turmoil.

If insecurity persists, quality of life suffers. When stress is inescapable people succumb to a long list of symptoms that affect normal functioning, including poor digestion, insomnia, anxiety, irritation, and so on. Since everyone feels the same work pressure, this constant confrontation makes everyone defensive. Proud and more arrogant types will feel impatient and take daring risks. Their frustration with the situation will make them tense and aggressive and they will seek to externalize their discomfort by disempowering others and finding fault in everything they do. Their victims will feel exhausted and oppressed by round after round of continuous submission, and depression may soon consume them. They will certainly lose their confidence and energy, isolating themselves from their colleagues. Eventually, they become martyrs to pessimism, operating about as far from abundance and well-being as possible.

The following chart maps our strategies when we are in the survival or conditioned mindset. It is divided into two sub-spaces and starts with our three essential reactions to danger.

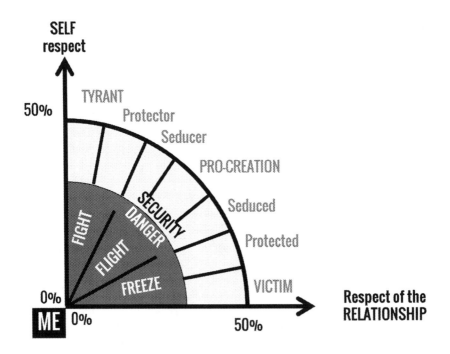

CHART 6: SURVIVAL STRATEGIES

Flight

"Tell them I'll call back tomorrow at ten am," said Yin, the CFO of a logistics company active in Africa. Government officials had visited a branch. They were furious and asked for several old documents. The local financial controller tried to reason with them, but given their ungodly attitude, he finally decided not to react to their request. Now, the inspectors had returned, threatened to block all the vehicles, and wanted to talk to the manager.

When danger threatens, our first response is to flee. Our body responds to our fear and prepares us for action, speeding up our heartbeat and respiration to deliver more oxygenated blood to the muscles. Digestion stops, our temperature rises, and we will even urinate if the danger is extreme.

At work, the threat is subtler. An email can make us react like we have a lion in front of us. The flight takes us away from the immediate threat so we can regroup. It gives us time to assess whether a confrontation is manageable and allows us to avoid low-priority requests or tasks beyond our control.

People who are overwhelmed because they tend to say yes to everyone don't get much benefit from the flight response. Their version is procrastination (you could say that they run away from their responsibilities) which leaves them feeling disempowered. Delaying tasks, blaming others, and silencing mistakes are typical flight behaviors.

Fight

"This is unfair!" Kathleen shouted at her boss. The project she had worked on for months had won the competition, but now it had been handed over to another department. Six months ago, she had been selected to participate in a Leadership program with twelve other high-potential middle managers. It culminated in a chance to present innovative ideas to top management, and they had promised to adopt the best project. Kathleen was bright, straight-talking, and hard-working. Growing up poor and jostling for recognition among four unruly brothers had made her tenacious. Her excellent grades earned her a scholarship to study abroad and her ambition was to climb the corporate ladder quickly, so she saw this presentation as a great chance to make a name for herself. But her boss had stepped in at the last minute and presented her project as if it was his own.

"Those were my ideas and this project won't happen without me!" she bellowed. A senior manager overheard the furor and called her the next day. She joined the project team two weeks later.

As this example illustrates, sometimes an angry response is entirely appropriate. Suppose there's no escape from an unjust situation. In that case, we can only attack, and just as lightning seeks discharge in the ground, anger can sometimes be the essential conduit through which our emotions find a resolution. When the storm requires quick, decisive, and sometimes unpopular decisions and actions, it must be expressed, and sometimes we just need to protect ourselves fiercely.

Shawn never knew his father. He was an only child who grew up in poverty. A tireless worker, he began his career by working three different jobs: a construction worker in the morning, a delivery truck driver in the afternoon, and a restaurant waiter at night. Mark, the boss of the construction company, quickly noticed his intelligence and ambition and took him under his wing. Fifteen years later, Shawn replaced him. Mark was proud because the two men understood each other very well. They were of the same caliber. Uncompromising, hard-working, detail-oriented, and completely lacking in empathy; only numbers mattered to them. Their employees all knew what "Come to my office," meant. It was either a telling-off or the door. The company had grown by reputation. Deadlines were met at all costs. The arrival of COVID and subsequent delivery problems put tremendous pressure on everyone and Shawn frequently got upset.

Consequently, they were shedding staff; two experienced foremen had already gone and it wouldn't be long before others joined them. Debtors were delaying payments. Cash flow was more of a trickle.

The fight response can become disruptive if consumed by it because controlling, fear-inspiring bosses are ineffective. When results are our only measure of success and we strive to achieve goals without regard for the environment or the situation of the people we work with, there will be casualties.

We lose our team's trust and commitment when we take credit for good results and blame others for bad outcomes. When we surround ourselves with people who are as combative as us and find it difficult to trust others, we will struggle to build productive working relationships. The more we worry about our survival and safety, the more risk-averse we become.

Being self-concerned and thinking we are all powerful allow anger to overwhelm us. We lose touch with the frontline experience and judge reality instead of understanding it. We become indifferent to losing people who have had enough and we can no longer control everything we are responsible for. Separating, manipulating, and blaming others for all that is going wrong block our capacity to respond quickly and with agility to new challenges.

Freeze

It's Monday, eleven am in London, the press conference is scheduled for the following week. The executive committee meets to discuss it.

"It's OK, everyone is ready for Monday," the CEO says.

"We said there would be no layoffs, but I just heard we're shutting down the Casandra project, which employs 25 people," says Steve, the attorney, before a heated discussion ensues between him and the CFO.

Kirsty, the director of marketing and sales, stayed calm, too calm. Casandra was her idea. She wanted to develop the Dubai market and had set up a team there. Sales did not take off as planned because of the persistent real estate crisis, and the local partner no longer felt in tune with the group. Indeed, the board of directors and the CEO had made sarcastic remarks about the Muslim community. Kirsty took offense and spoke briefly with her Dubaian partner. The press conference was about a new real estate complex in the UK, but the group's image had suffered recently. The Dubai reorganization had to remain low-key.

"Are you okay with that, Kirsty?" asked Steve.

"Yes," she said simply.

It was a whispered yes. Two months later, Kirsty submitted her resignation.

If we can't change the situation, we will suppress our feelings. This internal pressure will increase our stressability. We look dejected and weary, our energy weakens, and our gaze turns downwards. We feel the sensation of oppression like a weight in our chest and want to escape into isolation. But this isn't a true escape, and it only leads to an amalgam of unpleasant emotions, such as disgust, guilt, and sadness. The consequences are frustration, poor self-image, loss of self-confidence, rumination, and depression. Our thoughts become a constant narrative of negative beliefs: *"I can't do it. I can't change anything. There's no point,"* etc.

Alarmingly, the majority of the workforce uses this strategy. Globally, only twenty-one percent of employees are engaged, while sixty percent are not engaged and nineteen percent are actively disengaged, according to a Gallup poll in 2022. This means that most employees do not give their companies their hearts and minds. They prefer to fly under the radar, give only their time and minimal effort, and avoid seeking additional opportunities and responsibilities. The actively disengaged are similar but also hold grudges, complain about everything, and want to leave.

Constantly feeling unsafe is extremely draining and harmful. We need a secure place to function both in and out of work, so we seek refuge in a family, clan, group of friends, community, or organization. Once safe, we implement seven strategies to structure the group and ensure its continuity. We recognize alpha males and females. Relations between dominant and dominated groups are signaled using looks, posture, verbal and physical aggression, self-confidence, initiative, and charisma. All these behaviors are automatic and unconscious.

Pro-Create

Baby boom recorded during COVID

More children were born in Switzerland last year than at any time in the past fifty years

—Newspaper Headlines in April 2022

"It's amazing. The reservations are full. As soon as the borders reopened, our hotel regulars rushed back. And we're not the only ones who have noticed. Every luxury hotel on the island sees the same thing," said Colin, COO of Island Resorts Group. "I thought we would slowly pick up our pace after almost two years of closure. Now I'm having a serious problem getting staff back. Many have left the industry, and others don't want to work as much as they used to."

After the danger passes, our instinct is to procreate. For a business, **pro-create** means maintaining the status quo. There is pressure to do more of what we have been doing without questioning why or how we do it, simply because we have been doing it for a long time. We know this only works in a stable business environment, but not so well when disruptive storms hit us.

Seduce

I am tired of these long flights. "Why am I still accepting this kind of request?" As I register in New York's Park Central, I'm thinking to myself. The room is modern, and I like the bathroom's Andy Warhol painting style. It's too early to sleep. I go downstairs to have a drink. Two men are talking at the bar. A beautiful brunette woman dressed in the same red as the chairs plays with her phone two stools away. I watch them. She turns to look at me. Her red lips have too much filler, and perhaps she reads this on my face. One of the two men leaves. Obviously, they have just met. The other one drains his glass, catches sight of her and before long they end up talking, completely engrossed in each other.

Seduction is the oldest of the persuasive arts. Nature perfected it millions of years ago, and it's practiced today by amorous eagles, avaricious advertisers, and almost everything else alive. It isn't just about sex, though. As individuals, we might seduce others to gain protection, money, promotion, privilege, or any other prize you can name. We use physical displays, flattery, gifts, and more to subtly convince another person that we are each worthy of the other's high regard.

"Congratulations, you have won the lottery!" said the caller.

"Wow, and I didn't even buy a ticket!" I said as I hung up.

Every manipulative sales call is a seduction, albeit a relatively crude one. Others are more sophisticated, for example, drug companies have been known to hold conferences in exotic locations and offer all-expenses-paid places to doctors in the hope that they will be more likely to prescribe their latest medications. But whether it's advertisers trying to make you feel special or the company inviting you to join a group of high-potential managers, all these techniques seduce their targets by engaging their egos because our survival instinct is doubly satisfied. On the one hand, it helps members integrate into a group; on the other, it convinces them that the group has value.

Letting Ourselves Be Seduced

I arrive in Coimbatore. Krishan, the CEO welcomes me at the airport. I am honored. The Group headquarters asked me to conduct an audit and recommendations following a significant theft discovered by the new CEO who is having difficulty being accepted. Krishan is very friendly. He invites me to his home, and his wife gives me a beautiful cashmere shawl when I arrive. We talk about his family, his interests, and his professional situation. He comes from the north of India. For him, the Tamils are cunning and malicious. He discovered a network of employees who had developed an ingenious method of getting goods out of the factory without them being recorded in the accounts. Now that he has fired the people responsible, he is on guard. Not being from the same ethnic community, he feels isolated. He is afraid of not meeting his production goals because of the distrust between him and his management team. He knows I am close to his boss and asks me many questions. Every evening, he surprises me with the gifts he drops off at my hotel. A ticket to a concert, a guide for a city tour, and an invitation to a business lunch at his country club. At the end of my stay, I returned home and presented the beautiful shawl to my wife, then gave my assessment of the situation to Krishan's boss. I told him that while Krishan appeared to be complacent, I recommended giving him time to build trust with his teams before pressuring him on the numbers.

Two years later, the group had to part ways with Krishan. He may have seduced many people, including me, with his charm and generosity. Still, he hadn't been able to seduce his team and the production figures into improving to a satisfactory level.

Krishan's is an example of using a skill to achieve the wrong ends. Seduction itself is not bad as it's a way to open the door for a more trustful conversation, but if the relationship stays superficial, it backfires. In many cultures, business still relies on elaborate and protracted courtship games to build trust. No offense to anyone, but it's like foreplay. Get it right and it leads to fireworks, but overuse it, as Krishnan did, and you'll only manage to screw yourself.

Protect

Vivian was new to the finance department. Her clothes and tattoos contrasted with the more conservative style of the rest of the team. "She's here for an internship," Cecile murmured mockingly, "I don't think she'll last long." Although isolated, Vivian wasn't bothered by her colleagues' harassment. She had endured worse. She had run away from home at 13 and lived by her wits alone. No one knew it but Christian, the CFO, had a similar background, and now he wants to nurture Viviane toward success just as a concerned mentor nurtured him. He sees in her the same determination and knows she has the mental, intellectual, and interpersonal capacities to become an excellent resource for the company. It's a gamble that only the HR director and the CEO know about at present.

A leader is also a protector of their employees. He or she must make them feel safe and secure within the team. Identifying an employee with development potential and watching them grow gives a healthy sense of pride and is part of the leader's responsibilities. I have often observed that some talent developers see themselves in those promising employees they trust, encourage, and train. While this may seem unfair and biased, it is a normal and instinctive reaction. Anyone fortunate enough to have this kind of natural mentor is very grateful for it.

Françoise's two children are now at university and she is very lonely in her Paris apartment. Like her mother, she has spent her whole life serving her family. "I left Jacques, my husband. He said he had never loved me. Even though I did everything to make him love me, I was never good enough for him. He thinks I don't know anything about real life and I'll never be able to make money from my painting classes." A beautiful woman, she had married a young, ambitious entrepreneur who was divorced. She was indeed very carefree and temperamental when she was young. Spoiled by her parents, she had no degree and did not work much. The first years without children were filled with parties and trips. Jacques worked a lot, and she was always available to follow him. With the arrival of the children, she had to stay at home, often alone. She started to drink and even had a few affairs.

Sometime before Françoise's call, Jacques had told me his story. "My first wife had cheated on me and left me. It took me two years to get over the shock. When I met Françoise, she was lost. She had just arrived from the province. Her boyfriend had left her, and she was crying all the time. We spent five hours on the phone, and I saw that she had a good heart. I told myself that I was going to save her. 'At least she won't cheat on me', I thought, but the opposite happened."

Jacques had not understood the reasons and lessons of his first divorce. It took a second one to finally make him face himself.

Protecting others for the group's good is a necessary and beneficial action. But when we are triggered by our wounds and use others to protect ourselves, it becomes perverse and creates conflictual and even toxic relationships. Great leaders must be able to see the difference and help those who are wounded to work on themselves before they can protect others.

Letting Ourselves Be Protected

"I can't stand Heng anymore," said Peter, head of the Printing and Converting business unit. The SAP engineers had just received a delayed penalty and argued that Heng's team did not support them in integrating the former Sheet-fed and Web-fed business units to work with the same SAP software. In the past, both units operated independently and had their own IT systems. The Web-fed BU worked closely with SAP while the Sheet-fed BU was working with Oracle. The latter had developed several specific solutions they were very proud of, especially Heng, its IT manager.

Heng had arrived in France at the age of twelve, fleeing the Khmer Rouge in Cambodia. He was welcomed by a family who owned a big chunk of shares in this printing equipment and services group. After brilliant results in his computer management studies, he joined the sheet-fed company and gradually worked his way up to the IT manager position. He is a cold and self-confident technician, and over the years, he has earned a reputation as an untouchable. There are several stories of former colleagues who were fired because of him. "He is always complaining about SAP and does not implement the agreed changes. Now he needs to stop taking us for fools," Peter said. Heads would roll, but which ones?

In some companies, most often family-owned or governmental ones, we can find "protected" people resisting changes. Some are protected for their political connections, others for family reasons. Relations with these people are biased and can be very difficult to live with. They are the immovable object against which our reasonable and motivational approach will often fail. The more our suggestions push them out of their safety zone, the more they will block us, ignore us, and do everything to eliminate us. The only way to move forward will be to make them allies.

This was the fourth time I had seen the same three people laughing together in the cafeteria. "Who are they?" I asked the CEO of the African national airline. "Don't they have jobs to do, how can they be on break all the time?" "Ah, they are political protégés sent by our ministers. I can't get anything out of them. They spend their days running errands in town and wait for their salaries and free airline tickets for their families."

I tell myself that their days must be pretty unpleasant with all the envious or frustrated looks they must receive. I can see why they regularly leave their offices. "I have an idea," I said. "Christmas is coming and everyone will have to go shopping. Ask them to shop for your employees. It will keep them busy, and they will be serving the whole team."

"That went really well," the CEO told me a few weeks later. "Everyone was really surprised when I shared your idea, but since they shopped for the team the relationship has completely changed. The three of them have even started helping colleagues they never talked to before."

Dictate

When I ask people to name the greatest leaders in history, people often give me the same answers: Gandhi, Mandela, Martin Luther King, Mother Theresa, and sometimes Winston Churchill, Abraham Lincoln, Napoleon Bonaparte, George Washington, or Lew Kuan Yew. They rarely mention Hitler, Mao, Stalin, or Pol Pot, yet these despots motivated millions to kill others. They may have been atrocious human beings, but when you consider that most people don't want to kill anybody for any reason, the sheer scale of each one's atrociousness stands as an incredible if abjectly abhorrent feat of leadership. So how did they manage to wield so much influence?

When the storm comes, the human ego seeks a dominant figure. When the world is in chaos we can easily be swayed by inflammatory speeches from demagogues who have long been good at blaming people from different races, religions, or nations for all our misfortunes. It's no coincidence that fascism grows in popularity when people's lives are made harder. Charismatic leaders tell them they will restore their dignity and take back what's been 'stolen' from them. They are often arrogant people who like to impose their will on others. Typically, they don't tolerate criticism, are quick to judge, always think they're right, and blame everyone but themselves for their failures. They will gladly lie to cover their tracks and bully others to get the upper hand. They confide in their allies and project their emotions onto others until their followers end up believing that the leader's emotions are their own. They encourage others to feel guilty by pointing out every minor fault, even if they have nothing to do with the situation. They criticize and judge others in their absence and aren't shy about venting their frustrations.

We have all met leaders with this kind of toxic narcissism. They are easy to identify when they have power over us, but we will find it more difficult when we are in the leadership seat as they conceal their worst traits from us. Being a tough leader is mandatory for great leaders, and this is unpleasant for some in the short term. The difference between a toxic dictator and a great and challenging leader only becomes apparent over time. We only discover which one they were with hindsight by looking at their long-term results. Such people must ultimately be measured not by their behaviors but by their performance. When we look at them, we have to ask whether their methods have respected the company's purpose and value system, increased revenue growth, reduced absenteeism, developed promising colleagues, improved or impeded engagement, innovation, agility, or other essential factors. Everyone, good or bad, has to make the "right" decisions for the business. The following chapters will help us do that.

Play The Victim

This last survival strategy is probably the most difficult to accept because it generates ethically unacceptable behavior.

In 1947, African American social psychologists Kenneth Clark and Mamie Phipps Clark showed black children between the ages of six and nine two dolls that were exactly the same – except one was black and one was white. They would then ask the children a series of questions about the dolls, questions like…"Show me the doll that you like to play with … show me the doll that's a nice doll … show me the doll that's a bad doll." The majority of children ended up choosing the white doll as the good doll and the black doll as the bad doll. This experiment was repeated many times, and these segregated judgments based on skin color are still observed today. In several countries, most colored individuals have a lower sense of their own self-esteem and worth than those with whiter skin.

Different forces, such as peer pressure and social conditioning, will influence the relational positioning of some people and put them in a position of inferiority or victimhood vis-à-vis the dominant ones. This survival strategy is widespread in the workplace too. A recent Gallup engagement survey found that 19% of the global workforce is actively disengaged, and 60% is not engaged. As great leaders, we must understand and accept this fact. All sorts of factors precondition many employees to play the victim and complain. Although victimhood is often conditioned from birth and reinforced by unfair systems (such as those set up by a population who fear losing their privileges to migrants and other cultural groups) victims can escape it in adulthood if they know how to enter into the abundance mindset. Of course, we should change these systems through education, implementation of values, and exemplarity, but this shouldn't be our main focus. Our energy should be put into implementing strategies to grow abundance.

Stephen Covey once asked an audience of thousands, "How many of you seriously believe that the majority of your organization's workforce has more talent, more ability, and more creativity than their current job requires or even allows them to use?" Most raised their hands. "Now, how many feel pressured to produce more for less?" The same hands went up again.

How can we waste such resources and so much potential happiness?

I have an answer: we are asleep and letting our egos manage our lives.

Fortunately, storms will always come to wake us and force us to evolve, and we can also learn and educate ourselves to be better prepared, which is precisely what you are doing now. Congratulations!

Let's do a quick introspection. Pause for a moment and think of some complicated relationships you are involved in. Now think about the ten strategies that we have looked at so far. Which ones do you use to manage the different people in these relationships? Do you use more than one? When do you use them? The more you can take a step back and watch yourself handling these complicated interactions, the more awareness you will have of your reactive habits, which should give you more control over them.

These strategies may be good for maintaining your existing relationships, but they are not creative enough to help you manage the rapidly evolving disruptions that today's chief executives face. You will need other strategies to successfully grow in the unknown and generate abundance in these stormier waters.

The Ten Strategies to Grow Abundance

To transform my relationship with others, I must transform my relationship with myself. After that, it takes care of itself!

—Will Schutz.

When we're trying to survive, our priority is ourselves, and when others are trying to survive, they are only concerned with their own needs, which can make us mistrustful of them. But if we want to influence others positively, we must trust them first. If we start with the assumption that their intentions are good and demonstrate our trust in them then we have a much better chance of influencing them. When I practice this approach, I have found that people don't see me as a threat and are more likely to listen to my words.

To continue my map of human relationships, you will see in the diagram below that I have divided the spaces of abundance into three zones. The first is when I take the time to observe what is around me and within me. The second is where I decide to trust, and the third is where I let go completely.

You may also notice that the names on the axes have changed. Self-respect becomes assertiveness, which is the ability to express and defend one's needs without infringing on those of others. Respect for relationships becomes altruism, which is the ability to care about the needs of others selflessly.

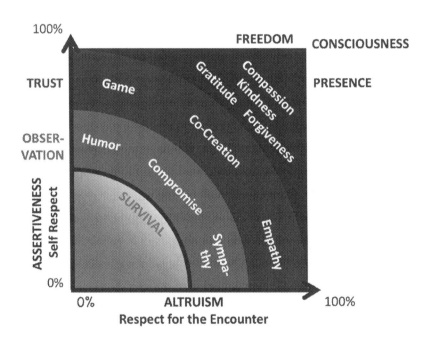

CHART 7: STRATEGIES FOR ABUNDANCE

MARC-ANTOINE TSCHOPP

Humor

Everyone has stopped talking. The tension is at its peak after two hours of this meeting. The agenda was clear, with an hour and a half to discuss: 1. Securing the right to union training for all workers. 2. Maintaining full pay during union training. 3. Replacement of employees during union training.

Three people represent each side. Robin, the CEO; Jeff, the lawyer; and Nath, the HR Director, sit on one side of the table; Mario, Andrew, and Margaret sit on the other. The relationship has been cordial and constructive for several years. Mario has been with the company for about thirty years. He is an empathetic and sociable person who is always concerned about the welfare of everyone. His opinions are listened to and followed by many employees, even those who aren't unionized. Andrew's nickname is "Baloo," after the Jungle Book character. At over six feet tall and 300 pounds he's someone you don't want to annoy. Mario and Andrew have represented the union for about ten years. Margaret is new. She's a relatively quiet person with a law degree and a master's in conflict resolution. Relationships have changed a bit since she arrived. Robin, Jeff, and Nath have agreed to accept all three requests. The question now is who will approve the training.

"I think all employees, union or not, have the right to take the training. It's helpful and fair for everyone to know their rights and duties," says Nath, and everyone agrees. "In this case, it is enough to follow the normal procedure, that is, an employee sees his direct supervisor to plan the training, then HR validates and manages it," she continues.

"No way, we get to choose who attends the training sessions," Margaret says, almost shouting.

"She's right, we should choose," adds Baloo.

"I don't understand why, everyone is entitled to it, right?" Nath wonders aloud.

"The union created these pieces of training," Margaret retorts, "You have to pay for it!"

"I thought our membership fees were going to cover it. We've been paying in 50% for years," replies Nath.

"It's true, we have had several meetings about it," Jeff confirms.

"Not about these courses," Margaret replies, then the debate fades away. Robin and Mario remain silent and seem to be counting the blows that Margaret and Baloo have been leveling at Nath and Jeff.

Then a heavy silence sets in and the four combatants quietly seethe. Mario looks sad, but Robin seems amused. He waits for the end, leans back in his chair, lets a wide smile spread across his lips, and says, "Well done," bursting into laughter. Mario follows suit five seconds later, then it is Baloo's turn, and Nath and Jeff quickly join them. Margaret is the only one who maintains her composure. Robin understands that she wants to maintain control over who can attend training to increase the union's power. He would have preferred to avoid this awkward confrontation. All three requests are accepted, and the standard training application procedure is maintained.

Humor is a natural strategy for lightening the mood, and at the same time, expressing profound truths. The ability to de-dramatize a situation, remain calm, and find connections makes people smile. It's not about being a comedian, telling jokes, and making others laugh. It's about laughing at ourselves to recognize how ridiculous we are becoming. That was the role of medieval court jesters. They were the only ones allowed to make fun of their rulers, bursting their bubbles of pomposity and speaking the truths that no one else dared to tell them. Today, the press cartoonists, stand-ups, and satirists fill their shoes.

The humor strategy isn't about simply making fun of people. Instead, we're discussing something inclusive that frees us from the ego's grip and invites others to do the same.

Smiling is a compelling means of communication. As demonstrated by Dr. Madan Kataria in his "laughter yoga" classes, the simple fact of deciding to laugh triggers a series of automatic reactions. Smiling quickly becomes contagious; everyone we meet will naturally smile back and relax.

Anyone who travels in countries with a Buddhist tradition or certain "underdeveloped" countries will undoubtedly have noticed this phenomenon. The people we meet in the street smile and laugh easily among themselves, even though their lives may be troubled and precarious. Their daily challenges are more perilous than most people endure in so-called developed countries, yet many are never short of a smile.

It has been established that a good mood can help us to succeed. Sonja Lyubomirsky, professor in the Department of Psychology at the University of California, Riverside and author of *The How of Happiness: A Scientific Approach to Getting the Life You Want*, and and her colleagues examined the correlation between happiness and success. By measuring the level of happiness before and after a successful experience, such as earning money or receiving praise, the researchers showed that it is not success that generates happiness. It's the other way round: happiness and a good mood are essential precursors to success. Success is a consequence of a good mood, not a cause. Happy people have other traits that facilitate success, too. Still, there is no doubt that a positive mindset leads to greater motivation and cooperation with those around us, which naturally smooths the way toward success.

Sympathize

During the G20 summit on April 4, 2011, Barack Obama arrived at Downing Street for the second time in three days. He was scheduled to meet with Gordon Brown as the UK and US faced demands from other world leaders for significant progress on financial regulation.

Brown greets Obama on the porch. Both head for the door where a police officer is positioned. The bobby decides to take Barack Obama's outstretched hand, but when he tries the same good-natured breach of protocol with the British Prime Minister, Brown won't play, and breezes past him. Perhaps his mind was elsewhere, but it looked like arrogance to everyone watching.

Before a meeting with somebody you find difficult to deal with, try practicing this simple exercise: ask yourself, "Why am I looking forward to meeting this person?" and identify three to five qualities you like about him or her. It might take some time and you'll find that even your worst enemies have a reasonable number. You just have to decide to see them. Then, after the meeting, observe what surprises you. Did they behave more constructively than expected? Did they share some positive comments about you? Is your relationship better now than it was at the beginning of the conversation?

As soon as we turn our attention to another being and focus on connecting positively with them, we let go of our protective mechanisms and allow them to do the same.

Discovering what others have in common with us makes them seem more familiar, whether it's an emotion, physical appearance, ideas, history, or experience. We are always looking for the familiar, and we warm to those who mirror aspects of ourselves and our worldviews. Once we understand how we are alike, the other person's differences become less of a hurdle, and it helps us to become more interested in them. Reaching others begins with sympathy and ends with a better understanding of them, hopefully granting us a better understanding of ourselves along the way.

Compromise

"I just got the carpenter's bill. He's crazy. He's asking for fifty percent more than we budgeted for," the purchasing manager said. *"On top of that, there are delivery delays. It would be best if you went to see him,"* he told John, who was overseeing the construction of a new warehouse.

Because of COVID, there were significant delays, and several changes had to be made, including replacing the metal structures with wood. The original budget for the systems was $800,000. John estimated that now the cost was more like $one million.

John and the carpenter liked each other. They both had the same attention to detail and workmanship and spent late nights devising creative solutions to the day's problems.

The negotiation began with champagne. They celebrated the end of the project, then came the hard part. "We don't agree with the amount you charged us."

"What makes you say that?" the carpenter replied calmly.

"You did a great job and were very responsive to our requirements," John continued.

"Yes, I even had to make specific plans for each arch we installed," said the carpenter.

"Okay, but the estimate you gave us didn't mention that. You're the specialist. You gave us an all-inclusive quote for the arches," John replied.

"Yes, but it was more complicated than we expected, and you had us make modifications outside of the quote."

"I agree, but there's a big difference between $800,000 and $1,200,000. With all our changes, we can pay you $1,000,000." The negotiation continued, and they shook hands for $1,100,000.

Once humor and sympathy are present in the relationship, it becomes very natural to find compromises between different needs or intentions. We listen to each other's requirements voluntarily and make concessions to reach an agreement.

This negotiation space is known as the "zone of possible agreement or ZPA." It exists when a potential deal is more advantageous to both parties than other options. For example, if a couple wants to spend time together, and it happens to be the case that Mrs. likes romantic movies, and Mr. likes movies in general, both have a zone of possible agreement, but if he only likes action movies, there will be no agreement zone when it comes to movies.

This ZPA negotiation space is critical for reaching a compromise, but identifying a ZPA can take some time. It requires not taking oneself too seriously and sympathizing with others to mutually listen to our wishes and needs.

Negotiation courses teach us that to compromise we must identify alternatives. Roger Fisher and William Ury introduced the concept of the "best alternative to a negotiated agreement," which is the recommended course of action a party should take if no negotiated agreement is reached. Using our couple's example, if they get stuck on the idea of watching a movie, they can either watch their film alone or consider other activities. This will depend on the minimum requirements each person places on the relationship. Specifically, they will need to define its value by spending time together. Once the alternatives and minimum requirements are shared, it is easy to define an area of possible agreement and reach a compromise.

On the other hand, when our ego activates us, each side pretends to have a better alternative than the one it has, and neither side expresses its minimum demands. Only by interacting with humor and sympathy can the parties gradually combine their interests and find a mutually agreeable solution. In this way, both parties can "win," even if neither gets everything they initially thought they would as they usually divide the cake into equal parts. You want to pay hundred, I want to get hundred twenty. We finalize the deal at hundred ten.

Trust

Humor, sympathy, and compromise are strategies that anyone can apply. To practice the next ones, we need something more: trust. It is the root cause of all our emotional and behavioral reactions.

"Who do you trust the most?" I often ask people. Close relationships are the first type that they mention, people such as their parents, partners, children, and friends. Next come the co-workers, neighbors, and certain professions like firefighters, notaries, and maybe a few others (who are increasingly losing the public's trust) like doctors, bankers, lawyers, and priests." Then I ask, "Have you ever been alone on a trip, in a place where you didn't know anyone, and met someone from your home country or who spoke your language?"

Those who had been fortunate enough to bump into somebody familiar while in unfamiliar territory said they were quick to get acquainted and soon began sharing more than they might otherwise have done. They trusted a stranger and opened up to them because the strangeness of their surroundings made them more aware of their similarities. This all changed if they encountered them back home though. The stranger seemed familiar in a foreign place, and then foreign in a familiar place. Neither of them had changed, it was only the number of familiar souls around them that varied.

Finally, I ask, "Think of a time in your career when you learned the most, gave the most of yourself, and had the most satisfaction, even though the work was taxing. When has this happened to you?"

The most common answers are when people took on a new responsibility because someone believed in them. Someone placed their trust in the person even though they may have lacked specific skills, and they stood by them when they made mistakes.

To truly put the following abundance strategies into practice, we, too, must first offer our trust. But to share it, we must first trust ourselves, and to become trusting, we must know where our "true north" lies. We will come back to this in a later chapter.

Neuroscience teaches us that trust is not just the absence of distrust. The two have different physiological origins. When we feel distrustful, that is, in the survival space, our amygdala is activated. On the other hand, when we feel confident, it is the prefrontal cortex that gets involved. This is where we compare our desires and expectations with reality. The more similar they are, the more confident we feel.

When self-confidence is strong, we take responsibility for everything that happens to us. We do not blame anyone else. Whatever the circumstances, we understand that we control our emotions, thoughts, and conscious actions. We do not strive for perfection but constantly seek to improve ourselves. We do not speak ill of others and can comfortably enjoy a frank and deep exchange of ideas. We know how to say "no" and do not promise what we cannot deliver. We know how to care for ourselves mentally and physically. Our actions are consistent with our purpose, and we do not hesitate to ask for help when necessary. We see failures or trials as opportunities to learn. They serve to help us understand ourselves better. We evolve towards tremendous respect for ourselves.

Here are two exercises that help us to restore lost confidence. This is very useful for those who are going through a depressive phase. The intention is not to find the perfect answers but to stimulate our minds to think positively. So self-questioning regularly and letting the answers diffuse all day long is the right approach.

---

7 questions to ask yourself every day to boost your self-confidence

1. Do I feel my body and connect to the present?
2. Am I completely independent of any criticism, good or bad? And do I feel superior or inferior to anyone else?
3. Am I my own best friend? And do I love myself completely?
4. To what/whom do I say thank you for what was given to me yesterday?
5. What event do I look forward to today?
6. Am I fearless in the face of any challenge?
7. Today, will I take another step toward who I really am?

---

3 affirmations to say out loud every morning, ideally in front of a mirror

1. I choose to be self-confident, even if I don't know how right now!
2. I choose to love myself and to listen to my needs, even if I can't completely do it now!
3. I choose to (use the verb that suits you)..... even if I don't know how to do it right now!

Play

"Ouch, that hurts, don't tie me up so tight," Laura yelled, but Seb didn't care. She was his prisoner now. She was the first thief he had caught. "No escaping, I'm going to get the others," he replied before running off down the garden. Laura began to cry. Her father arrived and untied her. A few minutes later, it was Laura's turn to play cop. The crying was long forgotten. She ran around happily, shouting, "I'm going to find you."

If we look at Robin's story with Margaret, the unionist again, he had understood the game she wanted to play but decided not to get involved, so things didn't get out of hand. This powerful strategy requires one to be vigilant about the intent behind each role play.

"Integrity and team spirit," was the company founder's oft-repeated catchphrase. Following his death two years ago, his son-in-law sold the company to the CFBO group which has given it a new dynamism, and Roger, the fire safety systems salesman, is now breaking sales records. He regularly travels to Nigeria and has managed to secure new business independently. Stephanie, the internal auditor, tipped off Fred, the new CEO that a former partner of the CFBO group in Nigeria said that the company was involved in influence peddling. The group's practices regarding corruption are rigorous. No bribery, no influence peddling, period.

"I didn't give or receive anything for these transactions," Roger explained. "The old boss taught us that. Integrity means you don't touch corruption. Teamwork means you work with local contacts, and that's what I did."

"Yes, but this person is not very reputable. He's close to the government, and we think there's influence peddling going on here," Fred said.

"But I didn't give him any benefits other than terms of sale that improve based on his volume. It's not my fault he ordered immediately and got better terms than your former partner," Roger said in his defense.

"How did you meet him?" asked Fred calmly.

"At a reception of the France-Nigeria Economic Chamber. We hit it off, and he came back three days later to talk business with me."

"And what do you know about his activities?"

"He is obviously involved in many things and is well connected."

"Was he already in the fire safety business before he met you?"

"Not to my knowledge."

"See, that's the problem. Your client is buying our systems and selling them at a much higher price to the Nigerian government. They can do that because he knows somebody in the Ministry of Infrastructure. The margin he makes is then divided between them. I understand you want to keep going, but you must stop this business, it is against our corruption policy."

Roger was surprised. He stopped selling to his contact, but at the same time, he left the company. We know he is still working with his well-connected partner in Nigeria and now lives surrounded by bodyguards.

Once we stay calm and observe the situation, we can see who plays which role for what intent. In this case, Roger wanted to make sales, the Nigerian buyer and Roger wanted to make a quick buck, and Fred wanted to preserve the company's values. Each one acted according to their own True North.

Fred is in abundance, and his ethics are more valuable to him than sales. The other two are selfish and greedy. It's as simple as that.

When we were children, we knew how to play. We were not attached to any role and could change our emotional state from one minute to the next. Life was not serious then and our True Norths were simple, like: have fun, now!

You may remember the movie Catch Me If You Can, which is based on the life of Frank Abagnale Junior, the greatest counterfeiter of the 1960s. He was a grown man who never stopped playing childhood games. He impersonated a high school teacher, a co-pilot, a doctor, and a lawyer and fooled the world for many years. After serving his prison sentence, he became one of the world's foremost check forgery specialists, working with the FBI to help them catch the most ingenious forgers.

The movie industry is full of similar personalities. We see characters go through the stages of their lives, moving from one role to another: a gladiator becoming an emperor, a beast becoming kind, a beggar becoming a millionaire, a finance trader becoming a monk, and so on.

We all play many different roles, sometimes in the space of the same day. I can quickly go from respected work colleague to teenage reject and back, someone who never stops moving all day and then turns into a couch potato at home. The wealthiest guy in my neighborhood but one of the poorest in a five-star hotel. Someone who flies first class but loves roughing it in a tent on vacation. Someone who is all-powerful behind his desk as an administrative officer but who sits on the sidelines of his sports team.

Play is about remembering that life is constantly changing. We must remain agile and fully assume these momentary roles to take full advantage of this. Then, as soon as the situation changes, we can take on a new role without losing sight of our main intention. Knowing where we are in our relationship spaces helps us choose the right roles that lead us to our True North. The key is understanding and defining a conscious True North as we will see in the following chapter.

On December 10, 2008, during the subprime crisis, Bernard Madoff's sons announced that the world's largest hedge fund was a Ponzi scheme. For more than 20 years, Bernie had been able to deceive professional investors, banks, the regulator, and his family by offering superior returns thanks to his clients' $18 billion in new money. In addition to the 4,000 clients who were defrauded, he was sentenced to 150 years in prison, his wife was left homeless, one son committed suicide, and the other died of lymphoma.

The biggest fraudsters are excellent actors and are primarily White-collar-criminals. The nonviolent financial crimes that include Ponzi schemes, insider trading, fraud, identity theft, copyright infringement, and many more explain why approval and trust in businesspeople have eroded in public opinion. These fraudsters never face their victims and are masters of rationalization, capable of compartmentalizing their feelings and personal ethics, denying responsibility, and absolving themselves of guilt. Extraordinarily, many are just as surprised at their egregious behavior as anyone else once the game ends.

A great leader must quickly identify these fraudulent actors. As for the Protecting strategy, we need to differentiate between whether someone is acting toward a conscious, ethical, and shared True North, or if they are a slave to their wounded ego. Key people parading material objects to indicate a rapid increase in social position, power, or status require support in their evolution. Executives with low behavioral self-control who also tend to indulge in high-risk behaviors for instant gratification need to be managed. Narcissistic individuals looking for constant positive reinforcement from others and requesting exceptions to the rules must be called to order. Someone must play the bad guy. It is our role to be exemplary. It is nice to be the one who inspires, praises, drives, allocates, agrees, inaugurates, and promotes. Confronting, challenging, refusing, cutting, and dismissing are unpleasant role plays, but we need both approaches, and it is a question of finding the right balance between them. To thrive, I suggest a magical formula that positive psychologists have identified: 3:1 for three pleasant scenes for every one unpleasant one.

Life is a massive game in which we are infinitely small and limited pawns. To accept that events unfold despite our best efforts and toss us around like a nutshell on rapids, we need only observe children from four to twelve years old. They stop to look at the ants on the ground, which becomes a game. They meet at recess and invent games joyfully and naturally. As adults, we quickly forget this awareness and become severe, rigid, and vigilant, unfortunately, sometimes too much so.

To become aware of how much control we have over our lives, I invite you to take a pencil and a sheet of paper. Write down ten things you would like to see in your future and ten things you would not want to see. Then, behind each of these things, evaluate on a scale from 1 to 10 how certain you are that they will or will not happen.

Do you have any influence over these events? What did you do to be born where you were born, to have the parents, spouses, and children you have? What did you do to get the job, the home, and the friends you have? Yes, you have put in the effort, ambition, and intention, but how much of what you are experiencing was simply given to you by life? If like me, you conclude that you have received much without doing much, then you can provide free rein to that quality of generosity and goodness that resides in all of us.

Empathize

"You're late again. I'm sick of you."

"I'm sorry, chief. I had to take my grandmother to the hospital."

"This time it's your grandmother, last time it was your mother, and next time it will be your uncle. Get this through your head now, there will be no next time, and if there is, you'll be out the door."

"Sorry, I promise you, there will be no next time."

Two weeks later, I pick up Riccardo hitchhiking. His face tells me a tale of sadness and worry. That's it, I remember. He is the waiter from the restaurant where I went to eat with my wife the other night. He made an excellent impression on us. He was very friendly, smiling, and quick about his work, and on top of that, he advised us very well.

"I just got fired," he says.

I am surprised. Did he steal from the register?

"I need to find a job soon. My mother and grandmother are sick, and I'm the only one caring for them."

I'm suspicious, but something inside me tells me he's sincere. I decide to drive him to his house. He is embarrassed. Perhaps I am right to be suspicious. Maybe there is no truth to his story. But the more I look at this boy, the more I feel sympathy. I want to know for sure.

He gets out but I follow him discreetly. The neighborhood is gloomy and dirty. He stops in front of a tin house. He seems to hesitate, then enters.

A gentleman passes beside me. I ask him if he knows the family who lives in this shack. "Ah, it's a sad story. They used to live a little further away in the family house. When the husband died in an accident, the wife, mother, and son were thrown out on the street. She is sick and the in-laws can't afford to keep her," he said.

My hunch was correct. This boy was sincere. I managed to find him a job. He is now a master sommelier in a Michelin-starred restaurant, and his whole family is better off.

Empathy differs from sympathy in that we mirror and feel the emotions of others. By engaging with others in this way their story awakens similar stories in us and can let us experience their feelings with the same intensity. This process does not occur in sympathy. Therefore, it is sometimes painful to empathize with people experiencing unpleasant emotions, as is the case for some caregivers or social workers. They tend to identify with the experience of their caregivers and begin to feel similar emotions. This is also why some overly sensitive people tend to shut down and reject the unpleasant experiences of others to avoid being overwhelmed by them.

The strategy of empathy means taking the time to understand another person's reality and taking a genuine interest in their whole life. For managers and employees who prefer to separate their work and home lives, this can be a problem, but we each need to let our guard down a little if we are to listen effectively and comprehend someone else's joy and pain. The goal is not to be overwhelmed by it (because then we would be just as disabled by the pain as they are) but to be aware enough of what they are going through to help. In short, we must understand their reality. When we accept someone else's reality as they see it, we can begin to see ways to change it.

Empathy and kindness are linked because we need kindness to feel empathy. Kindness is the ability to put the needs of others before our own and to be selfless to those around us. It is a virtue of humanity that's also found in other social creatures.

Social networks are full of videos of animals performing acts of kindness towards their supposed opposites, such as dogs nuzzling cats or cats grooming birds. It is kindness that creates caring and healthy relationships. Kindness is doing good deeds for others without expecting anything in return, simply because we want the best for them. According to Tayyab Rashid and Afroze Anjum, psychologists at the University of Toronto, kind people find joy in giving and helping others, no matter how different they are.

Co-create

The cab stops longer than usual. I poke my head out the window and see a fallen tree in the middle of the street with men talking while they work out what to do. Children are fidgeting in the school bus next to it.

"I hate this country," says my colleague as the first raindrops signal the coming monsoon. The driver looks at me in the rearview mirror and shrugs because he can do nothing

"We're going to miss our plane," she adds, annoyed. Some bikers shout at each other. Everyone is waiting impatiently for help to arrive, knowing that the Indian services can take days. I feel a sense of frustration rising in me as I watch a young schoolboy get off the bus and walk toward the tree. He seems determined and puts his little arms on the trunk. He pushes, but nothing moves. I smile. Other scholars join him, laughing in the rain and making a game of who can push the tree the hardest. Then the biker on my left takes off his helmet and encourages the gloomy adults to join the children. Soon twenty people are heaving away and together they clear the road. Everyone is overjoyed and my driver turns around, smiling. We will not miss our flight.

Co-creation is the combination of collaboration and innovation. These two skills are vital to helping us adapt quickly to the current disruptions.

According to the following chart, we can distinguish five levels of collaboration. I invite you to identify at which level you operate according to the groups in which you intervene. It will help you clarify what concrete actions you must implement to access the next level.

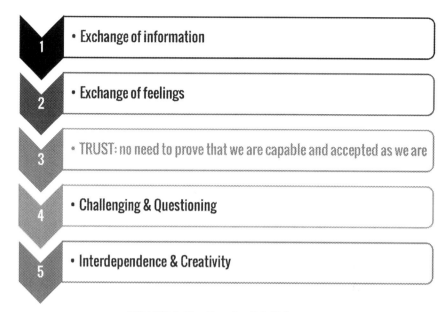

1 • Exchange of information

2 • Exchange of feelings

3 • TRUST: no need to prove that we are capable and accepted as we are

4 • Challenging & Questioning

5 • Interdependence & Creativity

CHART 8: Five Levels of Collaboration

The first level corresponds to formal working meetings. The agenda is repetitive. The leader leads the interactions, and everyone shares the information needed to make decisions, allocate those in charge, and set deadlines.

The atmosphere can be relaxed, and humor can be freely expressed, but to reach the second level, a sincere sharing of emotions is required. Knowing the emotion that a situation provokes helps us to understand the issues better and make better decisions. This is one of the reasons why emotional intelligence has become so important in the business world.

The third level is reached when the parties present genuinely trust each other. They no longer have to prove their competence and intention. Each party knows that the other is skilled and is doing its best.

The next level is co-creation, where everyone is concerned with the responsibilities of others and will challenge each other to make the best choice. The meetings are places of constructive confrontation. Disagreements are welcome and serve to evaluate situations from all angles. Once a decision is made, all parties adhere to it and speak the same language.

The last level is the one where everyone feels the flow. All actors are autonomous and responsible. The usual work is managed separately, and the parties meet spontaneously to settle exceptions and unforeseen events quickly, aware that each is independent and at the same time totally dependent on the others.

We need a safe space free from judgment and old beliefs to innovate. We have seen that humor and play can rescue us from unpleasant situations. They increase our self-confidence and stimulate our creativity. Empathy allows us to better understand what our clients, the public, or the market need because we understand their perspectives. Ideas and opinions can be exchanged confidently. Provocative confrontation and appreciative questioning help to lead everyone toward new possibilities. At these moments, the whole is greater than the sum of its parts.

The next three strategies are those of awakened or enlightened beings. We all experience this kind of state from time to time. The question is, how long does it last and how intense is it? In its purest form, this is the state of non-duality as defined by Buddhists. Hindus call it "Advaita," and some schools of thought call it cosmic or unified consciousness. I call this state "The space of presence, freedom, truth, compassion, and unity." While in it, our consciousness is anchored in the present. We are free, limitless, and blessed with huge capacity. We only express truth and authenticity. We feel connected and united with everything around us. We love all the beings we meet unconditionally. We offer forgiveness and gratitude spontaneously and sincerely. We use our intuition to discern things and pay attention to synchronicities. The flows of life and nature punctuate our actions. Abundance and gifts are our permanent companions.

Forgive

In 1992, South Africa closed the apartheid chapter of its history. While watching events unfold from my home in Switzerland, I believed that the black population would take revenge for all the abuses it had suffered over the previous fourty four years. I imagined there would be carnage, but this wasn't how it eventually played out. How did they manage to make peace? In 2000, I went to Cape Town and witnessed part of the "Truth and Reconciliation" process in Mandela's prison on Robben Island.

Three men sat on a podium, facing us. The one in the middle introduced himself as a judge. He would run this meeting. He began by giving the floor to the black man on his right.

"Tell your story," he said.

"I am a priest in Soweto, a black suburb southwest of Johannesburg that has seen several uprisings against apartheid. I don't have a place of worship, and my mission is to provide relief to families who lost a member during the uprisings."

Then in a deep, tired voice, he said, "I was shot at four times. The first time, I thought it was a mistake, after all, I was trying to help people. The second time, I realized I was the target. I was terrified and stayed home and didn't know what to do. After a while, I decided to continue with my duty. Every morning I would leave my family, saying goodbye, not knowing if I would return to them at night. I became very vigilant, but the fear was always in my stomach. The third time was another shock. Anger came over me, first at the police and the government, but also at my community and my leaders. The fourth time, I became angry at God. Why was he doing this to me? Why did I have to endure this unbearable ordeal?"

The judge then turned the floor to a white man sitting to his left.

"I was the one who shot at you."

"Yes," the judge replied, "tell your story!"

"I was a soldier. I carried out orders without knowing why or whom I was shooting at. I killed several people. Today, I realized that I took the lives of other humans. I am ashamed. I live in hiding in an old house in the bush. I don't dare look at myself in the mirror. I can't bear to see my own grandchildren. Please forgive me!"

The priest looked at him and said calmly, "It is not to me that you must ask forgiveness. It is to God... And I, too, ask for forgiveness." At this point, like most other observers, I was surprised. Why was he asking for forgiveness, this man who only became a victim by trying to help his neighbor?

The priest added, "I ask forgiveness for all the bad things I wanted to happen to you. For the anger I had towards you. For burying you in my mind to feed my pain. For the sleepless nights and the fears that came over me. For bruising my heart. I don't want it anymore. I want to be free. This belongs to my past, and I don't want to carry this burden any further. I only want to continue my path of love. The rest is your story. It's up to you to unravel it."

What a lesson that was! Forgiveness is not an act of omnipotence, where from the top of a pedestal, we deign to forgive the faults of others. It is an act of liberation, of unconditional love made in total awareness. It is done out of respect for ourselves and our relationship with others, from a space of presence.

"Forgiveness is not an occasional act. It is a permanent attitude," Martin Luther King taught.

"Every day, we wash our body of the impurities it has accumulated during the day, but what do we do to wash our hearts of all the emotional dirt it receives?" asks Olivier Clerc, founder of the International Association for Forgiveness.

Forgiveness is a personal act. We do it for ourselves, to free ourselves of some burden, and not out of obligation to anyone else. It is a healing process of the heart that allows us to regain our total capacity to love ourselves and to spread this love around us. It takes time and can only be done by being honest with ourselves. It is about "feeling" the need to free ourselves from a pain that has been with us for too long, and it starts in the head, with a conscious decision. Then comes the moment when our heart is ready. When, in every cell of our being, we feel this inner strength that cries out for love. It's not about forgetting, tolerating, or cozying up to the author of our wounds. It is about finding our power and our peace. It's about bringing what drives us all back to life when we connect to who we are. It is with this attitude that practical and healing justice can be done.

Express Gratitude

I am always surprised to see a waiter looking at me gratefully just because I say "thank you" when he serves me. This shouldn't be anything that's out of the ordinary for him, but sadly, it is. Most customers see him as little more than an invisible drone who makes food appear and he will only draw their attention if he makes a mistake, so the thank yous are a rare occurrence.

Imagine standing at the side of a road race and cheering on the runners as they pass by. Why do you do it? It's to lift their spirits and give them the strength to continue.

When they cross the finish line, people will congratulate the winners. Some say "Bravo!" and others say "Thank you." Who says which of them, and what is the difference between them? Everyone who wants a competitor to succeed will say "Well done," This group includes spectators, opponents, family, friends, and supporters. It is a free, kind, and generous act of love and joy.

Those who say "Thank you" also gain something. I'm thinking of his sponsors, team, coach, and maybe his banker. I'm exaggerating, of course, but my point is that when we say, "Thank you," to someone, we recognize that their act also serves us. We recognize that we are in a space of abundance together.

Several studies by positive psychologists have shown that expressing gratitude in this way is one of the most happiness-generating acts we can perform. Compared to groups that don't change their habits, those who write a daily gratitude journal are more optimistic about the week ahead and life as a whole. They are more enthusiastic, more determined, and more mindful. They spend more time exercising and have fewer symptoms of physical illness. They are also more likely to help others and make more progress toward achieving their personal goals.

Regularly reviewing our day in our heads before bed to identify all the gifts we received and say thank you to their authors helps us sleep more peacefully. Writing them down also anchors these acts in our minds and stimulates positive affect within us. It is so easy and so beneficial. We just need to focus on appreciating the little things we take for granted.

Be compassionate

"What advice can you give us?" a student asked Christine Lagarde, *Chairman of the European Central Bank.*

"We need self-confidence, and confidence is delivered by love," she replied. *"We need to invest in love. Off course, I say, work hard, travel the world, learn as many languages as possible, be receptive to other people, respect them, take risks in your life, inspire confidence, trust people more than you despise them, and give as much love as you can. A lot has to do with love. You must cultivate, nurture, and share it as much as possible. Then you will make your decisions and find your way."*

Some might find it strange that one of the world's most eminent bankers would mention love as the key to success, but to me, it's obvious, and we need this quality even more today. But what is love? There are different definitions depending on the state of mind we are in. If we behave according to our survival instinct, it is the energy used to seduce or be seduced, eventually adding to the species. This is romantic love. We identify with a loved one and willingly lose much of our power over our lives. All it takes is for the loved one to value us, and we feel transported, but if they reject us, we feel devastated.

Unconditional love means accepting others for who they are, the good and the bad. We usually have this kind of love for our children, to whom we are forgiving and accepting. Even though they may deceive, betray, or abuse us, we still love them, because we place no conditions on that love.

When we are in the survival space, we are vulnerable, so offering unconditional love then can be dangerous. We risk forgetting ourselves and our boundaries. The relationship can become unbalanced and invasive. We accept and feel obliged to respond to the other person's demands without expressing our own needs.

Compassion is the third definition of love. It lets us feel concerned for the person in front of us without feeling the weight of their suffering. We are present and support them with kindness, but without forgetting ourselves. To feel empathy, we must first be touched. But then, compassion is necessary to protect us from the negative emotions generated by the heart. Compassion is a feeling *for* the other, not *with* the other. Compassion stimulates ethical behavior. Respect for the rules of conduct and the values of a community becomes natural. We open ourselves to others without judging. We allow our humanity to express itself with serenity and confidence. We strengthen our bonds and increase our chances of survival. The ego relaxes, and our vulnerability is expressed without fear. The feeling of being different from others disappears. We can speak up, set boundaries, and make uncomfortable choices.

Olga Klimecki, a neuroscientist and psychologist at the University of Geneva Switzerland, has found that people with a high capacity for empathy are generally more aggressive, even toward those who do not threaten them. Conversely, more compassionate people are less aggressive, even toward those who have previously mistreated them.

When we look at the areas of the brain activated during compassion, we find that they differ significantly from those triggered by empathy. For empathy, it is the mirror neurons and their networks. They stimulate areas related to negative affective states and areas integrating information from the autonomic system. They are used for the acquisition of knowledge. On the other hand, compassion-activated regions are those related to attachment to the group, positive affective states, and those that manage reward processes.

When our heart is open and compassionate, we quickly connect to the state of presence. A feeling of total freedom washes over us, and the so-called unpleasant emotions pass through us instantly without leaving a mark on our being. We feel pleasant emotions without being burdened with pesky cravings or attachments. We think clearly and logically. Our physical sensations are fleeting and subtle. We feel happy and fulfilled. This is our natural state as humans. The one we see in children or animals. It strengthens our bonds within our community and increases our chances of survival. It opens our eyes to others and removes the impression that we are different from them.

Research shows that, among other things, more compassionate people have less anxiety and stress in their lives and are more curious, creative, willing, and motivated. In addition, they influence those around them to act more ethically and be more accountable. Compassion is contagious! If someone is kind and generous to us, it makes us want to be kind and helpful to someone else.

You can do an exercise with people you regularly conflict with, such as board members, partners, bankers, suppliers, customers, peers, employees, and family members. Do this discreetly before you meet them and use visualization.

While focusing on this person, repeat to yourself:

1. Like me, he/she is looking for happiness in his/her life.
2. Like me, he/she tries to avoid suffering in his/her life.
3. Like me, he/she experiences fear and the need to survive.
4. Like me, he/she experiences anger, arrogance, and mistrust.
5. Like me, he/she experiences sadness, loneliness, and despair.
6. Like me, he/she is just trying to satisfy his/her needs.
7. Like me, he/she is evolving on his/her life path.
8. Like me, he/she sometimes needs to be encouraged.

THE COMPASS

1ˢᵗ Step: PAUSE

Relax, Time; you are so beautiful.

—Goethe.

In my journey, I have long sought to develop those qualities of awareness, presence, compassion, freedom, and connection that I observed in the sages I met. I first tried to understand what these terms meant. I practiced heart opening, meditation, emotional expression, and energy release and found that I could touch this wisdom. However, this wisdom disappeared as soon as I returned to my daily life, with my professional commitments, family responsibilities, and social obligations. I waited with a certain impatience to find a better solution. I was looking for either a new master or more accurate and profound teaching, but I came to understand that these qualities were something that I already possessed. It wasn't a matter of acquiring something new but of liberating something, I already had to the fullest. Perhaps it's the same for you.

I have found that we can acquire skills simply because circumstances forced us to. Think of a time in your career when you learned a lot and felt very proud. Did someone push you into a new project that you didn't have all the skills for? This made you dig deep, and you discovered that you could handle it. In addition, you worked faster, processed a lot of new information, made quick and bold decisions, and somehow knew you were doing the right thing. The confidence you received from someone you respect gave you wings, and you quickly found yourself in a state of abundance.

These days, I coach groups of people to be more authentic and efficient at work and in their everyday lives, but time and again, I find that they already know everything they need to. The topics I discussed in the previous three chapters are nothing new to them, and they already have these qualities within them. I don't add anything to their knowledge but permit them to rediscover forgotten things. My primary role is to create a space of abundance quickly; with my map's help, it's easy.

I introduce some humor to help the participants relax and then encourage them to share honest and positive feedback about each other. Once people feel safe and have received praise, awareness and developmental commitments naturally and sincerely fall into place. This works well in classes or during coaching sessions, but, just as I do, when it's time to practice their newly revealed skills in the tension of their natural environments, many participants find this challenging and return to their survival space.

Little by little, I developed a formula to help us move from the survival space to the abundance space. It started as Stop, Observe, and Decide, evolved into Pause, Observe and Decide to be happy now, and ended up as PODnow®. It is a simple and effective tool that helps you reconnect to your omnipotence each time you realize that you are in the survival mindset.

The first letter, P stands for Pause. It doesn't mean "stop" in the sense of pushing away an unpleasant experience and blocking emotions. Pause is the first step towards elevation and awareness. It is manifested through silence, breathing, stepping back, and reaching equanimity. The practice of meditation teaches us to Pause and helps us to reinforce it.

Stay Silent

All answers are found in silence.

—Brother Dharmanand

Speech is silver, and silence is golden, or so the saying goes. Have you noticed that when we silently listen to other people talk, a quality of presence and power of awareness emerges in us? Some say it is the manifestation of the life force that animates us all. These characteristics disappear when we start talking again because speaking consumes your prana or life energy.

Antoine Papaloïzos was an original teacher. His psychology class was called "The Rule Game: Problems of Human Communication." During his lessons, we sat silently, observing each other for as long as possible. The tension would build quickly, the pressure of so many unspoken words became visible on everyone's faces, and finally, off came the masks! Then, in a clear and precise voice, one of us would explode with his truth, clearing the way for a robust exchange and a connection to our deepest needs and wounds.

Pausing, therefore, begins with silence. It is a gesture that can take many forms and last for various durations. We can use it to calm our survival reactions before acting. Here is a rough guide to practicing your silences:

- 3 seconds: Turn your tongue three times in your mouth, count to three, or be silent before responding
- 5 seconds: Look away from your screen before continuing to write
- 30 seconds: Get up from your chair and look out the window before responding to a problematic email
- 10 to 45 minutes: Meditate when getting out of bed or going to bed
- 30 minutes: Take a walk in nature to clear your head
- 7 hours: Sleep on an issue for one night before deciding what to do

Pausing is also very useful after becoming emotionally and mentally overwhelmed. It's about taking some time to reflect on what happened. We can try the following:

> - putting a subject, we are ruminating over down on paper.
> - talking with a confidante or coach about events that are disturbing us.
> - meditating on a question or a situation to connect to our wisdom and let our best answers emerge.

You have probably already tested these simple techniques, but have you noticed that the more you practice them, the quicker you get out of your survival space? More interestingly, have you observed that people around you follow your state change, and stress reduces rapidly for all?

Silence is probably one of the most powerful communication tools we have. Still, it's among the least trained, especially for leaders who need to inspire and implement change in a turbulent and chaotic environment. This book offers you several solutions to develop this ability. The first and simplest is to use your breath.

Breathe

There is a way to breathe that is to exhale shame and make us suffocate quickly.

There is another way which is to exhale a breath of love and open ourselves infinitely.

—Jalal Ad-Din Rumi

Connecting to our breath is a second easy way to get us out of the survival space. Our lungs regulate our vitality. While in a state of abundance, we breathe an average of 15,000 times a day, but when we are in survival mode, we can more than double this number. Our sympathetic nervous system secretes adrenaline and noradrenaline. Our heart rate increases and our bronchial tubes dilate. However, the volume of inspired air does not increase; instead, it becomes smaller and smaller, thus decreasing the gas exchange process. The importance of oxygen obtained with each breath remains low, causing hyperventilation. If these states become frequent, as is the case in a hostile environment or when we are in a "survival state of mind," our bodies will become increasingly fatigued. Our lungs will become accustomed to a low breathing volume, and we enter a vicious circle of "over breathing," generating physiological complications in the medium term.

After becoming aware of this chain reaction, we must relearn to exhale more intensely. Completely emptying the air in our body allows us to increase the air volume we can inhale and strengthens our lungs. This activates so-called abdominal breathing and naturally slows down the breathing rate. After a few minutes, our parasympathetic nervous system starts to work, and our heart rate decreases. Our bronchial tubes become compressed, and we secrete serotonin and acetylcholine.

Learning to breathe consciously is an exercise we can do anywhere, anytime, and it doesn't take very long. Various practitioners offer three-minute guided meditations on YouTube, which are worth a look. In general, there are three steps:

1. The first minute is spent answering the question, "How do I feel now?" This involves focusing on the emotions, thoughts, and physical sensations that arise and defining what is happening within you. For example, "I'm breathing fast... my breath is short...my throat is tight...my chess is tense...I don't feel like I can say what I need to say...I'm afraid of my co-worker's reactions... I feel nauseous."

2. The second minute is devoted to awareness of breathing. It is about feeling the air that enters and leaves our nostrils. To become aware of the sensations in our nose... the differences in temperature between the air that enters and the air that leaves... the natural duration of each breath in and out... we're just observing without trying to change anything.

3. The last minute is used for an expansion of attention. It is about gently focusing on the sensations that the breath causes in the throat... the lungs... the diaphragm... the stomach... the areas of tension and relaxation in our body... the quality of our emotions... and our thoughts... right here and now.

I like to wake up early, and when my kids were young, I made a point of coming home at night before they went to bed so I could see them at least once a day. As soon as I entered the house, they would come running happily, shouting, "Daddy, daddy." Tired from the trip, I asked them for a bit of patience, then I put my things in my office and wrote down the ideas that had come to me during my drive. When I came out a few minutes later, they were no longer interested in talking to me.

I felt misunderstood and disappointed. That's when I discovered www.heartmath.org and its cardiac coherence solutions. After this, I would come home, sit in my car for three to five minutes, breathe in coherence while listening to calming music, get out of my car, and be fully present for my children. To my great surprise, I realized that by practicing the same approach before a board meeting, a difficult conversation with my bankers, delivering a reprimand to an employee, or a tense negotiation with a supplier or client, I remained calmer, and my listening and argumentation skills were much better, too.

Recent discoveries in neurology have revealed that we have heart intelligence. When we connect to it, we access an intuitive source of wisdom. Perceptions become more precise and more expansive. All our senses are awakened. Our mental and emotional intelligence intensifies. We move out of the survival space and naturally enter the area of trust and compassion. We step back from our existing paradigms and beliefs, making our decisions straightforward and spontaneous.

We all know that a resting heart rate should be somewhere between 60 and 80 beats per minute, but did you know that in the same minute, our heart can beat at ninety bpm, then go down to forty bpm, and back up to seventy bpm, or go from sixty bpm to fifty five, then fifty, then back up to fifty five, then sixty, then sixty five and then back down to fifty and so on?

In the first series, our heart beats incoherently, which activates our sympathetic nervous system. In the second series, it beats coherently and activates our parasympathetic nervous system. If we learn to breathe coherently, we take full advantage of our lungs and heart. In all cultures, the heart is associated with love and relationships. When our hearts open, we feel unconditional love for ourselves and others, accepting everything and allowing us to build from this situation. Relationships become joyful, generous, and creative. These behaviors are particularly needed in stressful and disruptive environments as we are facing currently. But when our hearts are hurt, we create a shell to protect ourselves from further emotional injuries, thus limiting our capacity to feel or sense relational experiences.

The Heartmath Institute in California studies this heart intelligence and proposes several solutions to breathe in coherence. Here is how to quickly enter into coherence:

1. Take ten to twenty minutes to change your thoughts and feelings.
2. Gently concentrate on the area around your heart.

3. Breathe slowly and deeply (five seconds in - five seconds out), then inhale through the heart and exhale through the navel.
4. Think of a moment when you felt much love, joy, and gratitude. It could be a pleasant experience with someone close to you or a moment when you felt connected with nature. If you can't, place a smile or ray of sunshine in your heart area and feel how it relaxes, opens, and warms.
5. Make a sincere effort to keep this feeling conscious. If you are not experienced in meditation, your mind will quickly wander, and thoughts will "take over" your mental state.
6. When the mind wanders, focus on your breath, recall the pleasant experience, and become aware of the feelings of gratitude, joy, or love that come to you.
7. Ideally, listen to soft, pleasant music at the same time. You can download specific music at www.heartmath.org or music for synchronizing your cerebral hemispheres at www. monroeinstitut.org.

Many different types of breathwork are available, from simple techniques like the previous ones or easy yogic breathing exercises found in most wellness centers and applications like https://blacklotus. app/ breathe+, headspace, calm or waking up, to more complex ones like the www.wimhofmethod.com. I have personally tested many of them and suggest you try one that suits your way of living and is easy to implement, remembering that it's the practice that counts, not the technique or the application.

Take A Step Back

My method is different. I don't rush into actual work.
When I have a new idea, I start to materialize it in my
imagination. I improve it and make it work in my mind
before materializing anything.

—Goethe

In the 1980s, IBM commissioned a film from Charles and Ray Eames to demonstrate the relative sizes of objects in our universe. You can find this film on YouTube by searching for "The Power of Ten," although it has since been updated and adapted by various people. It is a journey that takes the viewer from the human scale to the infinitely large and the infinitely small. From a couple having a picnic, the camera pulls back and back to take in increasingly more significant areas, from our planet earth to the solar system, to our galaxy. It finally stops at hundred million light years and the billions of galaxies contained within that enormous diameter. Then the camera returns to its starting point and takes us in the opposite direction by first entering a pore of the picnicker's hand, then exploring smaller and smaller structures, including our cells, our DNA, a sidereal space composed of vacuum and atoms, the inside of an electron and finally a quark.

The first time I saw this video, I realized that the boundaries I set for myself were completely arbitrary and unnecessary. I thought my skin was the boundary of my body. I then realized that the person in front of me is also composed of DNA, atoms, quarks, or even vibrations, like every other thing, the banana I am eating, the table I am leaning on, and even the concrete of my building. I became aware of how we are all connected as our vibrations intertwine and go beyond the limits of our physical bodies. I also became aware of the infinitesimal impact my actions have in our universe and how I am influenced by everything around me that is larger than me. So why worry, why get angry, why believe my ego?

Nowadays, whenever adversity occurs, you can raise your head to the sky or look at the palm of your hand and smile. How will this adversity change the universe you live in? You know that your reactions will impact your vibrations, that's all. So it's up to you to choose whether to vibrate serenely or violently.

It Is Never Against You

Nothing other people do is because of you. It is because of themselves. All people live in their own dream, in their own mind.; they are in a completely different world from the one we live in.

—Don Miguel Ruiz

How often do we get into arguments with people we like or don't know? Remember the last time you came home from work late, and your spouse cooked you a nice meal? Perhaps you were greeted with, "What time do you call this?" and you may have replied, "You think I'm having fun? I work all day! How can we afford our kids' education or vacations if I don't?"

You might end up hearing, "It's always the same with you. I can't count on you!" You both endure a joyless meal, eaten in tense silence, and finish the evening watching separate screens with your arms folded. However, if you had taken the time to calmly reflect on what your spouse was saying, you would understand that they were looking forward to seeing you come home and sharing some quality time with you at the dinner table. Maybe they had something important to discuss with you. Who knows? But one thing you can be sure of is that if they were disappointed by your lateness, it was because they love you! If you had recognized this sign of affection, maybe you wouldn't have snapped back.

We experience the same reaction when an impatient driver honks at us, usually because we took half a second too long to respond to a green light. We recall our unpleasant thoughts about him when he speeds past us a few minutes later. But what do we know about his reality? For all we know he could be rushing to be at his child's bedside in the hospital, racing the clock to catch his plane, or perhaps he even has gum stuck to his gas pedal and can't slow down.

Coming up with three alternative explanations like this helps me to depersonalize the conflict, but then I can take it further by considering this:

> Everything the other person says or does to me is never AGAINST me. It is FOR them. I don't know what the FOR is, but my survival instinct is activated, and I tend to take what is happening as being AGAINST me.

As I focus on this idea, I remain silent. My emotionality quickly decreases, and my interest in the other person increases significantly. I try to understand what is good for them. In doing so, the other feels that the exchange is benevolent and changes his mood. We leave the survival space.

"Be the change you want to see," said Gandhi. This sentence is powerful because it quickly changes our mindset and is easy to implement. For instance, if I want to have a caring relationship with someone then I need to be calm and caring toward myself first.

It can feel harder to do this when we want a caring relationship with someone who may feel antagonistic toward us. Still, we need to remember that survival instinct can motivate other people to act impulsively. So, it's essential to be the first to step out of the abuser-victim-savior drama triangle as this can diffuse the situation. The benevolent leader begins by being compassionate to themself, as we will see in the following chapters.

2nd Step: OBSERVE

We should develop the power of concentration and detachment, and then with a perfect instrument, we can collect facts at will.

—Swami Vivekananda

The act of observing is natural for children. We are "like sponges" during the first years of our lives. For many months and years, we will scan our surroundings and copy the behavioral patterns of those around us. It is an act of love, and the looks of wonder in the eyes of very young children are so pure and present that we are enchanted. We spend much time carefully examining our external environment. Little by little, we define the limits and qualities of everything we encounter. Unconsciously, we build our synaptic patterns, mental representations, and beliefs. Then all too soon, the day arrives when we stop observing. We think we know it all—so there's no need to learn anything new. In our arrogant adolescence, we disdain everything that does not correspond to our understanding of the world.

Fortunately, life will always find ways to remind us of our ignorance. Trials will stimulate our vulnerability and force us to observe again. Devoting energy to looking carefully at what is happening inside us brings self-knowledge. Still, our hyperactive world leaves little room for this activity, so we must endeavor to make space for it.

This second abbreviation, "O," reminds us that we should seize every opportunity to make our observations.

Observe Your Physical Feelings

Hold out one arm and pinch yourself quickly and firmly with your hand. Do it several times. It hurts, and if you continue, it will hurt some more. The more you persist, the more you fight this pain, and the more tortuous it becomes... Now pinch your other arm with the same pressure as before, but don't let go of the pinch. Little by little, focus your attention on this pain. Try and inhabit it and ask yourself what these sensations are. Enter the sense and feel all its qualities. Does pain evolve to become less unpleasant? Don't you feel like you're just experiencing a different sensation and that you can get used to it?

The body is a very efficient measuring instrument. Like the engine temperature gauge on a car's dashboard, it allows us to recognize problems as soon as they appear because it tells us, so we don't have to wait until we reach the red. But to take correct readings of the dials on our body's dashboard, we need to pause from time to time and observe our behaviors.

In the following pages, I propose some guided meditation exercises for you. I encourage you to record yourself reciting them with a kind and firm tone. As you do so, aim to find the right balance between speaking and moments of silence. To do this, experience the meditations in your body simultaneously as you read.

Guided Meditation For Observing Our Physical Sensations

Special note for those who don't feel sensations in their body: before my Vipassana experience, I felt almost no sensation in my body. I had never paid attention to it, so it was something unknown. I know it's the same for many of us, especially those who activate their intellectual capacities and push their bodies to their physical limits. It takes pain or injury for them to feel something. If this is the case for you, instead of feeling, try to imagine the suggestions offered in my guided meditations. This works perfectly as well.

Find a place where you will be calm for the next 15 to 20 minutes. Sit comfortably cross-legged on a meditation cushion or chair with your feet on the floor. The important thing is to keep your back straight without creating tension or rigidity and to remain still throughout the meditation. If this is difficult for you, lie on your back with your palms up, your legs slightly apart, and your feet relaxed. If you need to adjust your position during the meditation, do so very gently. Anticipate each movement and execute it very conscientiously.

- I close my eyes and become aware of my breath, just as it is, without trying to change it. The air is coming in... The air is going out... Gently, I breathe out a little longer... and let my breath come in naturally... A second time... And a third time. Now I feel my nose and cheeks drawing in as I inhale and releasing as I exhale.

- Now... I focus my attention on one of my toes as it starts to vibrate or heat up... then I turn my attention to the other toe, which does the same... I feel this sensation all over the soles of my feet... They relax, and I imagine energetic roots growing from them and penetrating the ground... They are quietly spreading in our nourishing earth...

- Firmly anchored, I feel a wave of vibration that rises and relaxes the whole of my feet... I place my attention on my feet... I follow my feet and inhabit each internal space of my feet...

- This vibration continues to rise... It relaxes my heels... my calves... my shins... my knees... I feel the inside of each of my knees... They settle at the same time and create spaces... I follow my knees and inhabit each internal space of my knees...

- The vibration continues to rise and relaxes the top of my thighs... then the back of my thighs... and now my buttocks... which are gently but firmly resting on this chair or the floor... I lean even more on our earth... I focus on the perineum, the space between my anus and genitals. The vibration is soft and powerful... I taste this energy that circulates in me... this link that unites me with mother earth...

- Then the vibration enters my hips... they relax simultaneously... my prostate or my ovaries relax... spaces are created... powerful and profound energy circulates... I taste the qualities of my sexual gender... I follow this sexual power and inhabit each internal space of my pelvis...

- The vibration goes up... my colon and intestines relax... spaces are created between my navel and my kidneys... dense and courageous energy flows... I am this power, and I inhabit my navel and my kidneys...

- The vibration continues to rise... my abdomen... my solar plexus... and my heart relax... spaces gently open between my ribs and my spine... a loving, caring energy flows through me... it radiates all around me... I am this radiance... this link that unites me with all living beings in nature...

- The vibration rises... my lungs... my shoulder blades... my shoulders... my arms... my elbows... my forearms... my wrists... my hands... my fingers relax together...

- My neck and nape relax... spaces open in my throat... vocal and musical energy flows... I follow this sound vibration... this ability to express myself... to share my needs...

- The vibration rises again... my jaws... my chin... my mouth... my nose... my ears... the back of my skull... my temples... my eyes relax... a subtle, flowing energy circulates between my eyes and the inside of my brain... around my pineal gland, in the center of my brain... I am that flowing knowledge... I am the fruit of all my knowledge...

- My forehead... and the top of my skull relax... I taste this burning and serene energy emanating from the top of my head... it unites me to the universe, to my source...

- Now I connect to my whole body... from head to toe... my breath is peaceful... it nourishes all the spaces of my body... I become aware that I am larger... I radiate... I taste its vibrations... I inhabit my temple... I am my body... completely present... I am who I really am...

- Calmly, when I feel ready or willing... I breathe out profoundly... I stretch my hands... my feet... my arms... my legs... I open my mouth wide... I open my eyes... I stand up quietly... I slowly stand in front of a mirror... I smile at myself... I say thank you... thank you... thank you... and I hug myself with my arms crossed over my shoulders...

Observe Our Emotions

After the 2008 financial crisis, as most of my clients canceled or postponed my assignments, I decided to realize the professional dream I was afraid to start: creating a happiness center. As soon as I launched it, I was convinced it was right. The day put me in a state of fluidity and joy. My creativity was flowing, and I felt buoyed by something more significant. But the nights made me tired, and the anxiety weighed heavily on my sternum and stomach. The sales were not going well, but the costs were still there. My savings were melting a little more each month and paying salaries became a nightmare. I was strong and wanted to keep the teams motivated. I had to keep going. The fruits would come one day.

Little by little, sleep was becoming difficult, so I asked a doctor friend to prescribe me sleeping pills. He was concerned and sent me to a psychiatrist colleague.

"I'll keep you in the hospital for three weeks. You are severely depressed," was his verdict. I was in shock. I couldn't leave my business and family alone, but I realized I was carrying too much on my shoulders. I did not follow the proposed therapy but decided to close my business to concentrate on my family. The anxiety did not diminish; quite the opposite, in fact. What was I going to do next? How would I support my family? It felt like there was a bowling ball in my gut. One night, as I lay on my back, my vipassana meditation courses came back to mind. "Breathing and observing the sensations without being attached to them." I began focusing on this fear. Where was it in my body? How did it feel in me? I observed it and entered it. The sensations evolved and gave way to thoughts. Every day, I took pleasure in meeting this emotion. We became friends. It taught me who I was at that moment in my life and showed me the way to love myself.

During our daily lives, we experience various emotions that we sometimes call "feelings." These subjective states reflect the impact an experience has left on us. It is an energy or force conveyed by an automatic and expressive reaction. Emotions are a very effective form of communication that can be transmitted to others via various behaviors, such as tone of voice and body language.

Have you noticed that everyone else starts laughing when they see someone in a fit of giggles? Emotions are contagious and spread very quickly.

> Observe the next time someone angry walks into your workspace or a confined area and see what unconscious impact it will have on other people's emotions. You can do the same with a charismatic person.

If you are over thirty, do you remember exactly where you were when the two World Trade Center towers in New York City fell? Now, think about what you had for lunch three days ago. You probably found it easier to remember where you were over 20 years ago than what you ate three days ago! This is because emotion is a somatic marker. The more intense the emotional experience, the more we "store" the related information in our limbic brain. Adverts, movies, books, and more use this principle to try and make us experience strong emotions so that we notice, remember, and share them.

Of course, we are all different, so we will all feel different emotions in response to the same experience. How we react to it will depend on the sum of all our prior experiences and societal conditioning, meaning everything we've been through, and how we've accommodated it. As different as we are, certain human constants, such as the ability to produce and recognize emotional facial expressions, are universal. Researchers have demonstrated this by showing images of facial expressions to people worldwide, including indigenous communities. They all recognized the same primary emotions: anger, fear, sadness, disgust, shame, surprise, joy, and love.

"I feel cold with fear," "I was so angry, I saw red," "My heart is filled with sadness, "It sickened me to my stomach." We often describe emotions in ways like these, and Dr. Lauri Nummenmaa's team from the Aalto Faculty of Science in Finland has shown that locating them in particular parts of the body is a universal human trait.

The researchers asked seven hundred and one volunteers to look at stills and videos designed to arouse specific emotions. They then asked them to indicate where they felt them growing stronger or weaker on a human silhouette. These results confirm that people physically experience the primary human emotions of fear, anger, sadness, disgust, or happiness in the same way, regardless of where they were born.

Although we may feel the same emotions, the way that we are allowed to demonstrate them publicly varies between cultures. We should not show fear, sadness, or anger in business. In industrial countries, boys are dissuaded from crying or showing fear, but girls are encouraged to do so. Anger is sometimes tolerated when young boys are encouraged to demonstrate their warrior strength at recess. In some areas, such as southern Italy, widows must mourn and show their sadness if they want families to care for them.

Name Your Emotion

The easiest way to identify the emotion you are experiencing is to have a list of them at hand, then pause regularly and ask yourself which one you are experiencing at that moment. Here is a simple list. I suggest you copy it to your phone and play with it for a while. It's essential to get comfortable with this because expressing our emotions verbally rather than non-verbally will significantly improve our interpersonal communication.

> I strongly recommend that you take a picture of the
> following lists of emotions and have them handy
> on your phone to identify your emotions.

CONFIDENT	HAPPY	ALIVE	SERENE
Understood	Cheerful	Energetic	Centered
Open	Lucky	Liberated	Aligned
Reliable	Delighted	Optimist	In Integrity
Amused	Pleased	Provocative	Honorable
Free	Overjoyed	Impulsive	Stoic
Friendly	Content	Animated	Equanimous
Satisfied	Jubilant	Fragrant	Calm
Responsive	Fortunate	Thrilled	Peaceful
Accepted	Grateful	Frisky	At ease
Kind	Festive	Crazy	Relaxed
Surprised	Ecstatic	Vivid	Tranquil
Watchful	In a good mood	Wonderful	Composed

LOVED	INTERESTED	POSITIVE	POWERFUL
Blessed	Curious	Optimistic	Strong
Recognized	Fascinated	Upbeat	Sure
Considered	Intrigued	Radiant	Solid
Affectionate	Absorbed	Encouraged	Worthy
Passionate	Touched	Intelligent	Mighty
Admired	Attracted	Agile	Important
Valued	Concerned	Astute	Courageous
Cherished	Reassured	Good-humored	Brillant
Comforted	Honored	Buoyant	Influential
Adored	Meritorious	Caring	Relevant
Respected	Devoted	Determined	Unique
Favored	Captivated	Inspired	Perseverant

FEARFUL	ANGRY	SAD	GUILTY
Restless	Irritated	Pained	Sorry
Terrified	Enraged	Tearful	Responsible
Suspicious	Hostile	Chagrined	Defaulting
Anxious	Insulted	Unhappy	Blameworthy
Alarmed	Upset	Hopeless	Reprehensible
Panicked	Annoyed	Pessimistic	Punishable
Nervous	Upset	Isolated	Shameful
Scared	Offended	Distressed	Abject
Concerned	Aggressive	Dismayed	Crapulous
Shy	Bitter	Melancholic	Disgusting
Scared	Provoked	Gloomy	Unworthy
Worried	Inflamed	Inconsolable	Obnoxious

MARC-ANTOINE TSCHOPP

CONFUSED	POWERLESS	DEPRESSED	INDIFFERENT
Hesitant	Incapable	Shot down	Insensitive
Challenging	Paralyzed	Discouraged	Nonchalant
Uncertain	Tired	Demoralized	Neutral
Undecided	Useless	Lessened	Reserved
Perplexed	Inferior	Morose	Bored
Embarrassed	Vulnerable	Brooding	Cold
Disillusioned	Empty	Dark	Disinterested
Skeptical	Pathetic	Without energy	Stranger
Lost	Dominated	Moody	Refractory
Baffled	Stuck	Diminished	Jaded
Disbelieving	Fragile	Worthless	Carefree
Doubtful	Helpless	Sulky	Closed

Understand Your Emotions

We can divide emotions into three groups. The first type is a collection of the ones we express in the survival space, such as fear, anger, sadness, guilt, and disgust. We think of these as negative or unpleasant emotions because we experience them when our brains decide that we need to react to something unpleasant. They stimulate the secretion of cortisol which makes us withdraw into ourselves, stiffens our muscles in readiness for action, and increases our immune functions.

The second type is more positive and pleasant. These are the ones that we express when we are in an abundance state of mind, such as joy, sympathy, empathy, humor, forgiveness, gratitude, and love. They will stimulate the secretion of dopamine, which gives us the courage and energy to try new experiences, and oxytocin, which makes us sociable and helps us to develop intimate relationships.

The third group helps us to navigate between one group and another. It consists of pleasant and unpleasant surprises.

All these emotions are beneficial for our survival and evolution.

- **Fear** warns us when our safety zone is (or maybe) threatened. In other words, when someone or something threatens our physical, emotional, or mental health. For example: Alone at night, I fear someone following me might attack me.
- **Anger** gives us the energy to respond to the fact that our safety zone has been breached. For example, the person following me stands at my door, and I will call for help.
- **Surprise** helps to change my mindset: the stranger is, in fact, a neighbor.
- **Sadness** relieves the pain caused by the breach of our safety zone. It allows us to process our suffering after someone physically or emotionally attacks us. For example, feeling down after being robbed.
- Subtle emotions help us to restore some semblance of security. If the safety zone of a relationship is broken and we feel responsible, we will develop guilt. If we don't feel responsible, **shame** and **disgust** will emerge. These emotions are the breeding ground

for our traumas. Fear and anger allow the energy created by the stressful situation to be transformed into physical movements or vocal expressions. But shame, guilt, and self-loathing lock this energy inside our bodies. Over time, if we don't know how to "release" them, these energies will have unpleasant consequences on our physical, emotional, and energetic bodies. For example, I am angry at myself for being friends with this person but also angry at him for taking advantage of my friendship. I feel confused and worried about how to break off this abusive relationship.

- **Joy, surprise, and attraction** are possible when our safety zone is guaranteed and serves the species' reproduction. For example, weddings, parties, and end-of-year celebrations are often the occasion for meetings and seduction games between guests or colleagues.
- **Sympathy, empathy, and appreciation** reassure group members so they can rest and develop. For example, the leader who sincerely values and challenges his collaborator with the intent to progress and grow.
- **Contentment, serenity, and pride** show that our space is stable and comfortable. There is a balance among the group members.

Face Your Fear

Fear is our response to the possibility of something hurting us sooner or later. It could be a spider, snake, shark, airplane, the big boss, the taxman, the police, a disease, dying, or a million other examples. Some of our fears are shaped by our ancestral memories: spiders, snakes, and creepy crawlies tend to be universally reviled because of their potential to harm us.

The poor shark has been swimming with the pantheon of existing folk horrors that live in our collective imagination ever since the movie Jaws came out in 1975. Airplanes don't need such assistance. They are pressurized tubes spearing through the frozen air, 5 miles above the ground on four controlled explosions, and we are trapped inside them, wondering why the wings are bending so much. The board is all-powerful and can turn our good day into a bad one on a whim, as can the IRS, or the police, and disease is an invisible stalker that we can't anticipate.

All of these are real threats, but they become pervasive fears that we will do anything to avoid when we overestimate the likelihood of them happening.

We must first look at them head-on to overcome these and every other fear. That is, we must examine them with all our senses. Those familiar with spiders, snakes, and other insects know how useful, beautiful, and predictable they are. Those who dive among sharks know that only some of them, and in quite specific situations, can become dangerous to humans. Those who work with these boards know they are very human and respectful. Those who have gone through a tax audit know that there are specific rules to respect, and sometimes errors occur due to the increasing complexity of the declarations. Those who have had to deal with the police know that they are only doing their job and that they are mothers and fathers too.

If we want to calm all of our fears, we must first welcome them. We must observe them for what they are, without letting our strong emotional reactions and made-up stories color our view.

Here is a simple exercise for facing some of our primary fears:

1) Choose which of these three fears you want to work on now: your anxiety about money, your health, or your death. Then answer the following questions by writing them on a piece of paper.

2) Clarify your current state:

   - **Money**: How much do you make per month, per year? How much do you have readily available today? How much do you need per month, per year? To do what exactly? How much do you lack per month, per year?
   - **Health**: What is your current health status? What are your test results? How many different opinions have you gotten?
   - **Death**: What do you know about death and the dying process? If you have experienced a loved one dying, what was it like for them, especially during the last moments?

3) Close your eyes, think about what you have just written, and observe your body's physical reactions. Are there any tensions, pains, or tingling? Where are they? Linger with it for a moment.

4) Do the guided meditation for observing your physical sensations (see the previous exercise)

5) Project yourself 5 to 10 years into the future and answer the following questions:

   - What would you like to change that you are sure will happen?
   - What would you like to change that you are sure won't change?
   - What would you not like to change that is changing that you were sure wouldn't change?
   - What would you not want to change that you are sure will change?

6) Pause and breathe in coherence (see the previous chapter)

7) Reflect on your answers and observe how your physical sensations are changing

8) If you feel the situation is right for you, you can burn this paper while feeling awareness, compassion, and gratitude for yourself.

9) Take another sheet and project yourself into the next few weeks or months:

   - **Money**: What can you give up? How can you increase your income quickly?
   - **Health**: What are the next steps that will happen to you? How can you be sure? Have you met people who have recovered from this same disease? What exactly did they do? How can you best prepare yourself now?
   - **Death**: Have you accompanied someone at the end of their life? If not, go to a hospital for palliative care and accompany someone dying. Observe their questions, anger, and serenity as they leave. If so, did you follow them to the end? How did it happen? Did you talk with everyone? Did you have something to say? Remember, you have enough time to do whatever you need, so do it now.

10) End by hugging yourself and forgiving yourself for creating those fears that keep you from moving forward serenely on your life path.

Be Kind With Your Anger

Anger is an emotion that most of us keep in check. Every day we experience constraints and small adversities that feed our frustrations. Once we feel safe in our car or when we get home, we can let our anger out. Judging and yelling at unknown motorists is not so bad, but doing the same with our children, spouses, friends, or colleagues is going to be more consequential than hurting the feelings of a stranger in another vehicle. Anger is a natural response if we feel harassed, but harassing others only turns our problem into theirs.

Twisting our anger inward is equally problematic, but it can sometimes feel like the only solution when we know that diverting it outwards could jeopardize the relationship we have with our superiors, colleagues, or anyone else who influences us. Keeping this unexpressed energy locked inside us is no solution because it festers, which is why many people often succumb to the usual addictions of alcohol, drugs, sex, or work.

Here is a questionnaire and an exercise to bring our anger to light and to consciously welcome and transform it by creating new synaptic paths.

Assess Your Hidden Anger

	Please only check a behavior if you have experienced it		POINTS
1	Being preoccupied with tasks imposed on you until you have completed them		1
2	Being perpetually or very often late		1
3	Expressing humor in a mean or ironic way		2
4	Conversing in a sarcastic, cynical, or artificially light-hearted manner		2
5	Sighing frequently		1
6	Being overly polite, constantly jovial, and distracting		2
7	Smiling hurtfully		3
8	Having disturbing dreams or nightmares		2
9	Speaking in a controlled and monotonous manner		1
10	Having difficulty falling asleep, or trouble sleeping		1
11	Feeling bored, apathetic, or losing interest in things you normally enjoy		3
12	Performing your movements in slow motion		1
13	Being more tired than usual		1
14	Being overly irritated over small things		2
15	Falling asleep when it's not time		1
16	Sleeping more than you should, up to 12 or 14 hours a night		1
17	Waking up tired and not feeling rested and restored		1
18	Clenched jaws or grinding teeth, especially when sleeping		2

19	Having tics, spastic foot movements, clenching of fists, and other repetitive, unintentional, or unconscious physical manifestations		3
20	Being chronically depressed, going through long periods of depression for no apparent reason		3
21	Suffering from chronic stiffness or tension in the neck and shoulders		2
22	Suffering from a stomach ulcer		3
	Total points		

Analysis of results:

If you have less than 5 points, your hidden anger is low.

If you scored between 5 and 15 points, you are feeling anger. Do the following "Mirror your anger" exercise to free yourself from it. NB. You can go through this protocol several times.

If you have more than 15 points, you have a lot of stored anger. Perhaps you already do a physical activity to "let off steam." This is already very good, but more is needed. I invite you to find a coach and work on forgiveness.

Mirror Your Anger

On a piece of paper, list the names of all the people or organizations that generate anger in you, like your partner, boss, colleague, child, client, etc.

1. Write down the behaviors that stimulate this anger in you. (e.g., X complains and blames me for his problems; Y puts me down so he can shine in the eyes of others; Z abuses the power he has been given; etc.)

2. Once you have written the paper, reflect on each comment by asking yourself the following questions:

   i. How is this a message or gift to me? (e.g., X shows me that I, too, complain and do not take full responsibility for my actions; Y shows me that I, too, need to look good in the eyes of others; Z shows me that I, too, am sometimes smug and arrogant toward those I consider "inferior," etc.)

   ii. How has this helped me? e.g., Like X, I need to let go of some past frustrations or wounds. This awareness encourages me to be more accepting, more respectful, and more loving of myself as I am; Like Y, I need to be recognized and loved by others, and this invites me to respect them more; Like Z, I protect certain privileges or assets, and this encourages me to have more confidence in others and life.

3. Once you have spent some time reflecting on yourself, burn the paper.

4. Then hug and forgive yourself for creating these tensions and sufferings that close your heart and prevent you from shining.

Be Smart

I once asked a wise man what makes him different from the average person. He told me that some brilliant person might get angry just because someone "stole" the parking space they saw first. They then carry their anger around with them all day and share it with everyone they meet. Someone else may be mugged and resume their activities undisturbed after consciously exploring their anger. Wise people fall into the second category.

I often ask participants in my seminars to suggest the names of great leaders who have helped humanity, and three always come up: Gandhi, Mandela, and Mother Teresa. All of them have championed a cause related to self-respect. Gandhi and Mandela fought their oppressors so that their skin color alone would not define them. Mother Teresa invested herself in respecting the dignity of the most destitute, the Indian lepers.

Let us imagine ourselves as contemporaries of these great sages, starting with Gandhi. We are in a room with him, and he convinces us that we must demonstrate support for our rights in a non-violent way. To do this, we must stand in front of those abusing their power. Imagine walking down the street. About 500 meters away, there is a group of soldiers or policemen armed with batons and guns. Close your eyes and imagine the scene. You walk forward and see these men lined up in the distance, blocking the street. What is going on inside you? What emotion begins to overwhelm you? You keep walking. You arrive in front of these men. Their eyes are set. They are ready to use violence.

Again, explore the fear that grows inside you... One of them hits you across the head and drags you away. You end up in jail. A few days later, you are free again—explore how you feel. Gandhi asks you again to go and demonstrate. This is now the 20th time. Even though some of your friends have been seriously injured or are still in jail, how is your fear? You have probably overcome it, and it has turned into a strength. Fear no longer overwhelms you because you know it perfectly well. You are not afraid of anything anymore. This gives you enormous power, the power to stay calm when everybody around you might be fearful. That's what happened to Gandhi. A man without fear but full of compassion for all his fellow humans.

If we look at Mandela, who, after trying in vain to reason with abusers by appealing to the law, decided to use violence. He became a terrorist. Imagine how angry you would have to be to risk your own life and the lives of innocent people. Fortunately, he was caught and put in prison. He saw other "terrorists" arrive for twenty-seven years, full of anger and hate. He came to experience and understand the limits of anger. Later he said, "As I walked through the door to freedom, I knew that if I didn't leave behind all the anger, hatred, and bitterness, I would still be in prison."

He knew this emotion so well that when he stood in front of thousands of Africans chanting "revenge" in a stadium, he could calm them down "just" with his presence and powerful radiance. Imagine yourself in that stadium, surrounded by screams and hatred, immersed in that storm of violent energy. It takes a lot of awareness not to get caught up in it.

Mandela and others had the potent capacity to stay calm around people full of anger. It's a much-needed quality for today's leaders because it is easier to trick crowds into anger than bring them to reason. Mandela knew how to encourage forgiveness and reconciliation rather than bloodshed.

Mother Teresa transformed disgust into compassion. Imagine a beggar or a homeless person looking sick and filthy, lying on the ground before you. How would you react? Would you want to reach out to him, would you want to look away, or would you give him a coin? It takes a lot of awareness and love to see this person as a human being like us. We can all do it. By observing our emotions, and welcoming their extremes, we can escape our survival space.

When we hold our emotions inside, they accumulate and always end up "coming out," but unfortunately, at the wrong time, in the wrong place, and towards the wrong people. The accumulated energy will express itself violently and intensely like a volcano erupting, and of course, it is often considered inappropriate to express our emotions physically. Trembling with fear, crying with grief, or shouting with anger are not welcome behaviors at work, for example.

In the 1990s, Daniel Coleman, a journalist, and meditator went to interview the Dalai Lama. He wrote a world best-seller: Emotional Intelligence. Later, with other researchers, they defined the competencies related to emotional intelligence, and the business world integrated this science into its development programs.

Other researchers and psychologists like Marshall Rosenberg, the creator of Non-Violent Communication, propose to start a difficult conversation by sharing the emotion we are experiencing either just before an event that we think will provoke strong emotions in us, or afterward when we have had time to pause. When we express how we feel, we help the other person to unconsciously understand that everything that follows is not *against* them but *for* us.

The emotional quotient has replaced the intelligence quotient, and you can now pick from various EQ training resources. I don't claim that the following insights will replace these, but I regularly encounter them in my coaching, and they may enlighten you.

Emotional Intelligence is the ability to be aware of our emotions and their impact on our behavior. It starts with observing which emotion arises in which situation. Slowly it becomes easy to watch patterns emerge and act upon them. We then develop empathy to understand how others experience them and implement actions to manage our outbursts better. Once we have acquired these abilities, we can motivate, influence, and lead others positively.

Tame Your Moods

Psychologists discovered long ago that healthy people experience proportionately more pleasant emotions (those in the space of abundance) than unpleasant ones (those in the survival space). I have often read and heard that it takes three pleasant emotions to compensate for one unpleasant one. A scale developed in 1988 by Prof Watson of the University of Minnesota called PANAS (The Positive and Negative Affect Schedule) shows that the average person experiences two pleasant emotions for every unpleasant one. The happiest people experience four pleasant emotions for every unpleasant one, while depressed people experience less than one pleasant emotion for every unpleasant one. This observation has led many psychologists to suggest that for people with depression, it would be better to find ways to stimulate their experience of enjoyable moments rather than to give them medication.

So, to quickly change our emotional state, we need to focus our attention on something pleasant as soon as we experience an unpleasant emotion. We do this unconsciously when we snack or make impulsive purchases to compensate for our frustrations. More helpful alternatives include getting out into nature, doing an activity consistent with our values, or passing a rewarding message to someone around us.

Here is an exercise to help you develop emotional intelligence:

1. *Concentrate on positivity*: Without ignoring the opposing sides of life, avoid spending too much time around difficulties and challenges you can't deal with. Don't listen to the news, which primarily focuses on negativity. At work, cut it short when people discuss problems and put your energy into finding solutions instead.

2. *Surround yourself with positive people*: Don't listen to people who complain. Be aware that negative people drain our energy, so don't let them drain yours. Negative people learn to avoid positive people because they don't find a sympathetic ear for their complaints. Look for the positive in every situation and focus on the bright side of life.

3. *Smile*: Develop the habit of smiling and laughing, which attracts people with a similar outlook. Your charisma, open-mindedness, and caring attitude will make others see you as more trustworthy.

4. *Set boundaries and assert yourself*: Open-mindedness and a kind nature may appear easy prey for those who are more egotistical. Stay polite and firm at the same time by sharing your needs assertively. The best way to avoid making enemies is by adopting an alternative response when conflict arises. Think before you speak and give yourself time to calm an overblown emotion. If you can't say "no," say "yes and…" to open the door to other solutions. When in conflict, find a way to get to know each other better and start by sharing what you like about the other person. Then clarify that you both agree that you have a misalignment or misunderstanding and want to solve it. Before negotiating solutions, find the root causes of this situation and clarify your needs. Do not hold grudges or anger about how others treated you; instead, use the incident to prevent it from happening again. "Fool me once; shame on you. Fool me twice, shame on me," should be your motto. Forgive, but don't forget. If necessary, take a firm stand and bring those who have done wrong to account.

5. *Let go of the past, be conscious of the now, and focus on the future*: I know it's easier written than done, but one trick that works well here is to see gifts from life everywhere. A client's complaint is a gift that allows us to serve the next customer better. A failure may feel unpleasant, but it is an opportunity to learn a new skill. A challenge is not an obstacle but an exercise to strengthen our values.

6. *Be a lifelong learner*: Continually learn from the experiences of life. Grow and evolve, be open to new ideas, and always be ready to learn from others. As a critical thinker, be ready to

change your mind if someone comes up with a better idea. While being open to suggestions from others, trust your judgment to determine the best decision for you.

7. *Manage your energy*: Don't work too hard. Balance your life, spending quality time with your loved ones and yourself. Learn breathing techniques, take exercise, sleep well, eat healthily, and have fun every day.

Observe Your Thoughts

For a long time, the word meditation seemed incomplete to me. As a young student, my parents placed me in a boarding school run by Dominican monks. They regularly "invited" us to sit in the church to meditate in silence. I looked at the walls, wondered if what we were doing served religion, and thought of many other more exciting things, like the girls I wanted to attract or the games we would play afterward. Twenty-five years later, I read about Tibetan monks and their incredible physical, emotional, and intellectual capacities that they obtained in part through meditation. So, I decided to try it and signed up for a ten-day Vipassana course in silence taught by Goenkaji (www.dhamma.org). What an encounter with myself that was! What a wonderful gift.

After three days of concentrating on the air flowing right under my nose, I was invited to focus on the top of my skull. I felt like it was on fire. It burned like the head of a saint in a church painting—I was surprised to feel such intensity when I hadn't been conscious of anything a second before. I was then invited to go through my entire body and found that it hurt everywhere. How was this possible? One moment my back felt fine, and the next it was overflowing with intense sensations. This made me understand the power of attention and quickly illustrated what an essential mental attribute it is.

Little by little, I would learn to taste my sensations, welcome them, and observe how they transform from dense to fluid. Later, I lived a strange experience that I consider to be ecstasy. I was nothing but vibrations, a ball of energy. I was radiating, floating above the earth. I was not flying but was so light that I felt levitating. It felt great, and I didn't want to leave this state, but these sensations changed as soon as I craved it. The more I craved to go back to that previous state, the more my body became a rock, hyper-dense. I had to learn again to let go, to welcome what was. I became aware of impermanence. I was learning about life.

There are several meditative practices, and all of them try to calm the flow of our thoughts. A sincere prayer, where we put ourselves in a quiet place by closing our eyes and by abandoning ourselves to the messages that come from the depths of ourselves, is a form of meditation practiced in all religions.

Asia offers several very advanced practices. Some combine breathing and movements like Yoga, Chi-Gong, or Taiichi. Others work on our emotions like Shamatha, or our conditioning like Vipassana. Others use mantras or a series of syllables to be repeated in a prolonged way to reach a state of appeasement and modified consciousness, as in the case of transcendental meditation, which was very fashionable in the 1960s thanks to the Beatles and the Hippie movement. Others still deepen states of consciousness linked to death, like those practiced by Buddhist monks.

Practice Mindfulness

Mindfulness is a form of meditation that is in vogue today. It can be summarized as the practice and state of continuously being aware of our thoughts, feelings, and emotions. It is a way of being that is derived from the teachings of Siddhartha Gautama or Buddha. Its great advantage is that it can be practiced easily anywhere and anytime. No need to sit cross-legged for hours on end; just a minute's pause from time to time is a good start. It consists of bringing your attention back to the present moment and examining the sensations that come to mind, how they appear, how they last for a while, and how they disappear. This practice allows you to:

- become aware of the close link between our four qualities: body, emotions, thoughts, and soul.
- discover our thoughts and moods.
- learn to be present and appreciate the small pleasures of daily life.
- break the downward spiral that emerges from a wrong perspective or painful memories.
- "shift gears" to get out of hyperactivity and be more aware, more balanced, and less judgmental.
- accept ourselves as we are without worrying about the gazes of others or societal judgment.

Meditation greatly interests leaders and policymakers in today's hyperactive, stressful, competitive, and uncertain world. The aim is to help students, athletes, and employees become more effective and happier. Meditation has been shown to significantly improve concentration and memory, which like muscles, will become stronger the more we use them.

It also reduces anxiety. By increasing our conscious experience of an abundant state of mind, we weaken the neural links or myelin pathways used when we are in a state of survival. This mindful practice simultaneously strengthens the connection between our evaluation center (the part of our brain known for reasoning) and our bodily sensation and fear centers. So, when we feel frightening or upsetting sensations, we can more easily examine them rationally.

Meditation stimulates creativity and compassion as it decreases the frequency of Beta waves and increases Theta and Delta waves in our brain. This allows for the emergence of new ideas and a benevolent interconnection with each being.

It is about practice and goes through several states of attention, becoming increasingly sophisticated. At first, we quickly become aware of our thoughts wandering. Little by little, we manage to detach ourselves from this and focus on the object of our meditation, which could be our breathing, a mantra, our physical sensations, a flame, the space between us and a wall, etc., for a few seconds. With more practice, we become aware as soon as our mind wanders, but we do not let ourselves be disturbed. Only after thousands of hours can we completely pacify our minds to subtly observe ourselves and recognize our tenacity, carelessness, thoughts, emotions, and all other distractions while staying fully present for more than two hours.

The aim here is not to become a senior meditator but to train our minds to become more focused and calmer. This can be done with simple daily awareness sessions of 2 to 10 min, and phone apps can help you do this.

Identify The Stories We Tell Ourselves About Ourselves

Oscar's parents had separated when he was eight years old and his mother had to emigrate to find a low-paying job. He was soon forced to work to help feed himself and his little brother. His childhood wasn't a childhood at all. It was a nightmare where he was forced into a position of overwhelming responsibility way before he should've been.

He may have survived into adulthood, but he eventually reached a point of exhaustion. He divorced and realized that everything in his life was dark. He may have created a successful business and financed his children's education, but his life still felt like an endless nightmare. He constantly told himself that he had no right to happiness, but the day he met the woman who would become his next wife, she ended this thinking. She made him aware of his recurrent destructive thoughts, the source of his permanent malaise. Once he understood his patterns, he could make peace with his past and live happily and without guilt.

Identifying recurring thoughts is a task that requires patience, and the assistance of a good coach can be helpful. This is not necessarily a professional therapist but someone who knows how to listen and identify the stories we have been telling ourselves for a long time. These stories are the basis of our conditioned and limiting thoughts and activate our emotional outbursts.

Here is a simple exercise to identify our stories:

---

1. Take four sheets of paper and write in large letters:
   - Sheet 1: "I should not ..." – "I can't ..." – "I'm not capable of ..." – "I would have been better off if..."
   - Sheet 2: "I should have ..." – "I should not have done ..." – "I regret ..."
   - Sheet 3: "I should ..." – "I have to do ..." – "If I don't... I will ..."
   - Sheet 4: "Who am I without these stories?"

---

2. Use a recorder or have someone write down what you say.

3. Place the four sheets on the floor before you, not too close or far apart.

4. Stand in front of or on the "Who am I without these stories" sheet. Close your eyes. Concentrate on your breathing and exhale three long breaths. Then relax your feet, legs, stomach, back, chest, shoulders, arms, hands, and face. Mentally scan your body to look for tension, pain, or pressure. If you find some, breathe into that area. Once you are relaxed, enjoy this state of being for a few seconds. Enjoy how good and "normal" it feels.

5. Stand in front of or on the first sheet of paper, read, and complete the four sentences. Close your eyes and take your time. Also, try to remember what you told yourself as a child.

6. When you have said everything, come back to the "Who am I without these stories" sheet. Breathe calmly, look at where you are, listen to all the sounds, savor the smells, and relax. Feel this state of being again: who you are without the stories.

7. Stand in front of or on the second sheet of paper, read, and complete the three sentences. Close your eyes and take your time. Again, try to remember what you were already saying to yourself as a child.

8. When you have said everything, come back to the sheet, "Who am I without these stories." Breathe calmly, look where you are, listen to all the sounds, smell the smells, and relax. Taste this state of being again. Who you really are without the stories.

9. Go to the front or the third sheet, read and complete the three sentences. Close your eyes and take your time. Try to remember what you were already saying to yourself as a child.

10. When you have said everything, come back to the sheet, "Who am I without these stories." Breathe calmly, look around you, listen to all the sounds, smell the smells, and relax. Feel this state of being again, who you are without the stories.

11. Step out of the exercise and reread or replay your stories, trying to identify the most disturbing ones. Be cautious. They may overwhelm you emotionally and create tension or physical pain in your body.

Now that you have identified your stories, you can observe how much they occupy your thoughts. Over the next few days, whenever you feel discomfort or experiences overwhelm you, try to find out which thoughts are overwhelming you the most.

3rd Step: DECIDE

When we look at ourselves, we only see a form of desire for happiness, but not the DECISION to have this happiness permanently. Should we blame happiness or ourselves?

—Barbara, quoted by Maddly
Bamy, wife of Jacques Brel

During my childhood, I was influenced by my father's culture of traditional mountain farmers and my mother's world of refined and subtle artists. He powerfully instilled material values in us, and she opened our eyes to the immaterial world of beauty and finesse. I had the chance to live several contradictory experiences. I was immersed in the music of the Beatles and the film Woodstock, and I had created an ideal world full of peace and love. I dreamed of becoming a clown to make people laugh or a lawyer to save the misunderstood people of this world. But when I reached adolescence, I had a painful experience. Lost, misunderstood, and unable to achieve my childhood goals, I was consumed by a desire to disappear. I was, however, rather cheerful and sociable, but at that time, I thought I was being dragged into a way of life I did not want and could not leave. To be who I wanted to be, I thought I had no choice but to leave that life.

The belief that we don't have a choice creates enormous pressure. It is one of the leading causes of stress at work. Those stuck on this thought put themselves in a hellish prison, but it is a colossal illusion. We always have a choice, but perhaps not the courage to choose. Deciding to respect ourselves and take control after forgetting who we are for years seems unlikely, but the trials of life will often lead us to regain it and finally exercise our freedom of choice.

We can't decide what we feel, but we can choose how we react. We are not always aware of our actions' consequences, but we can respond or act consciously. It is a matter of mindset. The more we are subjected to conditioning, the less we are masters of our destinies.

"To choose is to give up," said André Gide. Our illusionary expectations are just dreams created by our ego. If we stay attached to them, we think we cannot choose or decide and remain stuck in languid and lasting suffering.

For a change to occur, there must be some unpleasantness, which means activating our survival space. Therefore, we start by avoiding, getting angry, or inhibiting the causes of these sufferings. Unfortunately, this does not help, and we will experience more unpleasant emotions and thoughts, such as guilt, shame, doubt, and loss of confidence. The longer we stay in this demoralizing energy, the less we can decide.

The pressure falls like a house of cards when we give up our conditional constructions of ideals and judgments. Although fears emerge, the new energy puts us into action and invites us to make other decisions to face the challenges.

You Always Have The Ability To Respond

Being responsible is a concept that needs to be understood more. I see that today, many people seek to avoid responsibility. Education leaves the family home and is transferred to the school. Teachers take refuge in protocols and unions to protect their actions. Patients expect medicine to cure their health problems. Insurers propose solutions for everything but negotiate hard when it comes to paying. At work, we cover ourselves by copying everyone in on emails we send. In politics, we entrust our power to those who promise much before the election but don't deliver and leave even heavier "baggage" for the elected officials who follow them. Victimization becomes commonplace, and the fear of an unpleasant future rumbles on.

But what does it mean to be responsible? Here are some everyday situations you may encounter.

A. You are on public transportation. An older adult you don't know is looking for a seat while two young teenagers have fun sitting right in front of them.
B. You are in a queue at a ticket office or checkout. A shameless person slips in between two people who are behind you.
C. At the office, an irate customer abuses a young colleague you do not know well. This colleague is not in your department.
D. You are going home tonight. As you arrive at your front door, right next to you, there is a ripped-open garbage bag. There is household waste on the sidewalk and the road, but not on your property.

Are you responsible for these situations? Most people I ask say, "No." Really? Put yourself in those first four situations and imagine your reactions. Look at your emotions. Do they feel angry, disgusted, or superior? Observe your thoughts. Are they judging these young teens, intruders, colleagues, clients, or neighbors?

Do your thoughts look like these? *Today's youth need to be better educated. People don't respect the rules of propriety. That colleague must not be very competent. That customer must be a pain in the ass. My neighbors are thoughtless...*

Also, observe how you tend to amplify and generalize your judgments with thoughts like these: *The parents and teachers of those teenagers are also to blame, and so are the people of different races or communities who don't respect our rules, the human resources department will hire anyone these days, and the garbage collectors don't come by often enough to pick up my garbage and the public authorities don't do their jobs properly...*

Imagine that you come home in this emotional state. Your child greets you with a worried look. They have just made a mistake or received a bad grade at school. How will you react? Will you get upset? Then your spouse asks you for a favor. How will you respond? Will you listen to them, or will you retaliate? How will you end the evening? Will you stay isolated on a couch in front of a screen with a glass of alcohol or meet with your family around a table to happily share a meal and stories?

All this because you were not responsible! As I mentioned before, responsibility is the ability to respond. An Indian sage named Sadhguru said that. He explains that we are accountable for everything that happens in our lives. That is, we can respond to whatever we become aware of. We are thus free to do what is suitable for us in the situations we encounter in our lives.

To repeat the examples above, imagine that in every situation, you say to yourself, "I am responsible for this, and I can choose to respond in whatever way I want to this reality."

A. You may smile at this older person and encourage him to ask the youth for a seat. You can ask the young people yourself calmly, knowing that they are just absorbed in their conversation and that they, too, will be happy to be of service to someone. You can also ask them firmly and mindfully to stand up.

B. You can turn around and thank the people who let this person pass between them because they must know them. You can even, with sincere humor, offer them your seat if they are in such a hurry. You can also ask this person to stand in line like everyone else, but without getting angry, just with confidence and assertiveness.

C. You can support your colleague by encouraging them to learn from their mistakes. You can stand right next to the customer with a kind smile to show them that you understand their difficulty and gently encourage them to calm down. You can even firmly ask the client to calm down.

D. You may go home quietly, as your priority is to spend quality time with your loved ones, but you might also choose to go and collect the garbage and encourage your neighbors to do something together to prevent this from happening again. You can call your children and have them help you pick up the trash to teach them the meaning of cleanliness. You can suggest a neighborhood meeting and invite everyone to clean up the trash together.

Now, look at your emotions. Are you calm, proud, joyful, and compassionate? And what are your thoughts? Do you play with life's events feeling free and creative? Do you see an opportunity to serve your community and help raise awareness? All this because you have decided to be responsible!

And what about those who have experienced or are experiencing an intense situation, such as:

- learning that you have a severe illness and that it is hereditary
- being harassed at work by your boss and colleagues
- being the victim of a burglary
- enduring domestic violence
- having been abused as a minor

Saying that you are responsible for any of these situations may offend you, and I fully understand. If this is the case for you now, I am sorry to trigger a deep-rooted wound and invite you to take a break.

Experiencing an ordeal of this intensity entrenches us enormously in our survival spaces. Since we cannot flee quickly, we can only fight or submit. We tend to position these realities outside of us by rejecting the physical sensations, emotions, and thoughts that invade us. Pain or fatigue might be treated by medicine, surgery, justice, or violence. Fear, anger, shame, guilt, and sadness are buried deep in our flesh. The incessant ruminations stun our minds: "Why me? It's unfair! I must be wrong; I must deserve it," and we resent ourselves, our loved ones, our ancestors, and society.

Those who have come to terms with these kinds of trials know this well. To transform them, we must accept responsibility before doing the right thing. To be responsible does not mean to be at fault but to act on the situation. When we make peace with the causes of our emotional disturbances, we can choose to free ourselves from them in the act of love and turn them into life lessons. To be responsible means working from the space of abundance. We will first find the most appropriate ways to respect ourselves in intense situations.

- We can listen to our intuition and dare to take medical and paramedical steps. We become friends with our physical sensations. We get in touch with ourselves and uncover long-hidden wounds. As epigenetics now explains, we understand that it is how we breathe, eat, move, sleep, welcome our emotions, let go of our thoughts or maintain our relationships that influence the activation of our genes. We can decide to change these behaviors and find the strength to do so over time.
- We can step back and learn how to protect ourselves better.
- We can free ourselves from unnecessary attachments to material possessions.
- We can reclaim our physical integrity by reconnecting with our dormant or deadened parts.
- We can seek help and reclaim our honor by daring to share our mishaps without anger, victimization, or the desire for revenge.
- We can stand up and face our abusers without fear or hatred.
- We can regain our freedom and heal our hearts by forgiving our abusers.
- We can bring them to justice to face the consequences of their actions.
- We can even see the pain in them and have compassion for them.

One of the difficulties with responsibility is the confusion between "being responsible" and "being accountable." Living in society requires us to live by standard rules and requires each person to respect the commitments made in the group's service. "To be accountable" means being ready to justify our actions and accept their consequences. If we fail to comply with the rules and commitments expected by society, we become punishable. In anticipation of this, we try to avoid it by protecting ourselves by all possible means. As events become more and more uncertain, complex, violent, and rapid, one of our first survival reactions is to avoid our responsibility by blaming others and to cover ourselves by giving our power to leaders, compliance committees, lawyers, therapists, gurus, and other saviors. Unfortunately, when we turn to them for help, we often find that they can't do much for us. Our frustration and sense of victimization hit their limits, and we feel lost. This is when addictions help us to numb the pain.

Choosing to exit such a vicious circle is the role of a true leader. We are totally responsible for the events and circumstances we encounter in our lives. Each trial is an opportunity to practice conscious leadership and continue to evolve.

Be Consistent With Yourself

Being responsible also means being consistent with ourselves, which is when our actions are "aligned" with our values. If we react from our survival space, then fear may push us to behave in a way that we wouldn't under normal circumstances, which is inconsistent with our stated values and beliefs. However, it reveals an important lesson: we still have lingering influences that would benefit from our attention.

When we decide to be responsible, we can better understand what we project onto others. We can look inside ourselves and identify the stories that we overlay reality with. Integrity prompts us to ask objective questions about the conflicts we experience, such as:

- What are the facts about what just happened?
- What emotions did the situation trigger in me?
- What initial judgments did I make?
- What parts of my personal history are being reactivated at this moment?
- Which of my latent or conscious needs is not being met?
- How can I thank the actors in this event for holding up a mirror that allowed me to meet a hidden or rejected part of my personality?

This book shows you how to enter the spaces of abundance and practice forgiveness, letting go, gratitude, and compassion. It contains many other initiatives to encourage you to take back your power.

Bruce S. Gordon, a successful business leader and president of the NAACP, grew so tired of receiving requests for help that he created the ladder of accountability, a simple tool to encourage people to become more responsible.

We use this tool when events are not going as planned, and we want to help someone face them with all their power. I encourage any parent or leader to teach this ladder to their children or subordinates. They can then come back and coach them up the ladder of responsibility, one rung after another.

It starts with teaching, educating, and knowledge sharing. If I ask a child to fix an electrical outlet or a trainee to sell a product, and I don't first train them how to do it, I can't hold them accountable for getting electrocuted or failing to make a sale. Without knowledge sharing, there can be no empowerment.

The following three levels are those of powerlessness or victimization.

1) Once trained or aware of the rules and commitments, the first tendency of those who do not feel responsible is to find someone to blame. They will use the most common phrase: "It's not my fault; it's...". I am often surprised by the ingenuity and sometimes the bad faith with which some people express themselves when they lean on this step.

2) Once they realize they can no longer shift the responsibility to others, they move to the ladder's second rung and use an excuse. This evasion sometimes takes the form of magnificent justifications or rocky alibis full of regret and self-flagellation.

3) The third level is more pernicious. It is the one used by anonymous victims of all kinds. This 30% of employees feel disengaged and unconsciously destroy the value of the company or group in which they are active. It is also the case for 50% of all citizens who hope something will change but do not vote. This is the attitude where we wait, counting on a possible messiah or miracle that will solve all our problems.

The following four levels are those of powerfulness, where engagement, empowerment, collaboration, co-creation, innovation, and freedom are activated.

4) Empowerment starts from the moment we share and acknowledge our different realities. We are in that space of caring communication where we can express our perceptions and needs knowing that the other is listening attentively and without judgment.

5) Once this exchange has occurred, we naturally assign roles to each other according to our professions, abilities, skills, or

inclinations. A constructive negotiation can take place and will serve as a support for future collaboration.

6) We then move on to a creativity phase, where the search for solutions and appreciative questioning will stimulate commitment, motivation, and delegation.

7) The last step is to record and follow up on our decisions.

This tool is simple and effective if steps 4) and 6) are carried out with patience and confidence. Remember that if you are not in the space of abundance, you will only activate the other person's survival mechanisms. At worst, the other person will become more and more efficient in his efforts to stay on the first three levels. He will use ingenuity and lousy faith to defend himself and sometimes use group or media pressure, as with some unions and tabloid journalists.

Trust Your Gut

We are all faced with choices, but how do we make the right decisions? I don't have any magic answers because I, too, have been stuck at an impasse and unable to make decisions on many occasions. But I realized that I was paralyzed because I feared losing something, and I also noticed that my biggest indecisions were the ones that would cost me the most, both emotionally and financially. But I started moving once I had stepped up and made a decision. Yes, I made mistakes, but I learned from them, adapted my actions, and moved on. It was always an opportunity to evolve.

As leaders, we know that making a decision is to risk failure, but it's only necessary that we fail less than we succeed, ideally at a rate of one mistake for every five or more successes. So how can we reduce this ratio?

When I hired Deniz, I didn't think he was ideal, but I felt pressured to find a guide who knew Istanbul. He ticked the right boxes as he spoke French, knew the city, and could educate us about Sufi philosophy. Expectations were high as we had little time and had invested a lot of money to learn as much as possible from this trip. We were delighted with the five-star hotel, the succulent food, and the city tour, but the promised Sufi experience with Deniz was an exercise in total frustration. He only knew about the subject from reading books, not from first-hand experience. I should have listened to my gut feeling.

How many times have you experienced a similar outcome? You knew the right thing to do but didn't act on your first impression. Many people aren't sure whether they should follow this initial insight. In his bestseller *Blink*, Malcolm Gladwell showed us how snap decisions often yield better results than careful analysis. Gerd Gigerenzer, one of the researchers of behavioral intuition responsible for the science behind Malcolm Gladwell's book, demonstrated that our gut feelings result from unconscious mental processes. The value of these unconscious rules lies precisely in their difference from rational analysis. By examining various decisions we make, Gigerenzer showed how gut feelings lead to good practical decisions and underlie the moral choices that make our society function.

Know How To Discern

When Pope Francis was elected, a journalist asked him about the qualities one should have to be Pope. He answered: "Discernment." "What is that?" continued the reporter. "Thousands of people will follow my decisions, and I need to be sure that what I decide comes from the Holy Spirit." He needs to lead the faithful to God and not to darkness. To succeed, he shared a two-step approach. First, he must reach out to the neediest. Those for whom the interval between life and death is very tenuous. It is in their presence that he understands Life. Second, he needs silence to pray and let the universal wisdom tell him what to do and how to do it.

You may have noticed that the advice to "sleep on it" when you have an important decision often turns out to be good. It certainly works for me when I wait a day to respond to a "provocative" email. That delay can make all the difference, partly because my morning meditations sometimes offer surprising ideas. Sleep itself can offer new perspectives for all of us because, during our deep sleep phases, we gather information from various parts of our "memory" that we then process during other phases of sleep phases. This might be why I trust my early morning messages and write them down soon after waking up.

Discernment is recognizing small details. The capacity to perceive subtle information is critical. All our senses need to be open, and the closer we are to those impacted by our choices, the better. Once gathered, we must process these details and accurately tell the difference between similar things. Silence and a clear mind are now essential. These skills should be trained constantly.

Don Miguel Ruiz, a Toltec nagual, said, "When you want to know if a thought is from God, you only have to check if it generates fear." If it does, you know it's coming from our conditioned mind. If it generates peace of mind and love, you know it's coming from a more significant source. Love is a concept that is starting to be accepted in the business world. Christine Lagarde, President of the European Central Bank, said recently, "We need to invest in love... we need to cultivate, nurture and share it as much as we can". In my understanding, love is the most potent human energy. It prevents the instrumentalization of fear. It releases confidence and establishes the calmness we need to face the future with positivity and commitment. Amid the turmoil, it sees all the possibilities and truly puts us in the service of life.

Knowing where to look for answers is a skill each conscious leader should possess. The Pope shows us that nourishing our consciousness by going closer to reality is crucial. We can't stay behind a screen, a phone, or a book to feed our brains with the subtle elements essential for a good decision. We must spend face-to-face time with our customers and employees to truly understand them. Once we have consciously and unconsciously gathered these pieces of information, we need time to digest them. Finally, we must evaluate solutions that accommodate our purpose, values, and needs. Understanding enough to "feel" the right choices brings us more peace of mind and love. As we can see, rational analysis is not enough. We must learn how to feel. This is why PAUSE and OBSERVE are essential steps we must take before DECIDING. But how should we decide? It took me years to come up with this simple answer: Decide to follow your true north!

THE TRUE NORTH

4th Step: LOVE YOURSELF FIRST

The day I loved myself for real, I understood that I was in the right place at the right time in all circumstances, and then, I could relax. Today, I know this is called Self-Esteem.

The day I loved myself for real, I saw that my anxiety and emotional pain were nothing more than signals that told me when I was going against my convictions. Today, I know this is called Authenticity.

The day I loved myself for real, I stopped wanting a different life and started to see that everything that happens to me contributes to my personal growth. Today, I know this is called Maturity.

The day I truly loved myself, I began to see the abuse in manipulating a situation, or a person, for the sole purpose of getting what I wanted, knowing full well that neither of us needed this. Today, I know this is called Respect.

The day I loved myself for real, I started to free myself from everything that was not beneficial to me, people, situations, and everything that lowered my energy. At first, my mind called this selfishness. Today, I know that this is called Clean Love.

The day I loved myself for real, I stopped being afraid of free time, and I stopped making big plans; I gave up the mega projects of the future. Today, I do what is right, what I like, when I like, and at my own pace. Today, I know that this is called Simplicity.

The day I loved myself for real, I stopped trying to be correct and realized how often I was wrong. Today, I have discovered Humility.

The day I loved myself for real, I stopped reliving the past and worrying about the future. Today, I live in the present, where all life happens. Today, I live one day at a time, and this is called Plenitude.

The day I loved myself, I understood that my head could deceive and disappoint me, but if I put it at the service of my heart, it could become a very precious ally.

—Kim & Alison McMillen

For fifty years, I tried to do the best I could to do the right thing. It meant following family, school, military, and societal rules and simultaneously listening to my inner voice. I enjoyed playing hooky and ignoring abusive orders, not to be contrary, because respect for human values was more important to me. This earned me punishments, betrayals, and even imprisonment, consequences that I did not understand. Deep questions arose when my little family and my new business started crumbling. I had done everything I thought was right, not for myself but for others, only to end up feeling unloved and unrecognized. I was alone, facing myself. If others couldn't love me, I realized that I would have to do it myself, but what does it mean to love yourself?

At that time, I didn't like myself. I was ashamed, disgusted, lost, and depressed. The change started with a decision. I wrote the following sentence on a Post-it note and stuck it on my bathroom mirror so that I would have to see it every morning and evening. It said, "I have decided to love myself even though I don't know how to do that yet."

I soon added another powerful ritual where I would say thank you for three things that had happened to me during the day that I was grateful for. Gradually, I became aware of what made me proud of myself. I was evolving and becoming less dependent on the behavior of others. A new journey of self-discovery began, offering me peace, joy, detachment, surprise, forgiveness, freedom, connection, and compassion.

If you want a quick exercise to see what loving yourself means for you now, imagine that next week will be eight days long. You get an extra day and can do anything you want. Please take a few seconds to think about this and list all the activities you would like to do on this bonus day.

Chances are, your answers are similar to the ones I get from the people I suggest this exercise to: take time to rest, cuddle, train, or spend time with people you care about but haven't gotten together with in a long time, like your parents, your friends, or yourself!

The fact that we all want similar things that we don't do enough of shows how much we all need to love ourselves more. We devote a lot of time to dealing with emergencies and the needs of those around us while believing that we will always be able to make time for ourselves later.

I have noticed that the things that I would do on an extra day can vary depending on my current state of mind. Still, unconsciously, I am always seeking to satisfy my ego and indulge my physical, emotional, and mental wants. These include eating and drinking, romantic moments, buying expensive goods, spoiling a loved one, or getting a relaxing massage. Many of my choices depend on the gazes of others, especially those who belong to the clan I want to be part of. It's important to me to look good, dress fashionably, drive a fancy car, have a recognized professional status, belong to groups of influential people, live in a trendy neighborhood, make the "front page" of newspapers, or receive many likes on social media.

But more profound wisdom can manifest when I pause and observe. I then know when my real needs and priorities are different. I feel my actions are not in line with my purpose and they invite me to seek answers to the following six questions:

1. Who am I?
2. Where do I come from?
3. Where do I go?
4. Why am I here?
5. How do I want to behave?
6. What should I do?

Find Your Masters

We were separated into two groups, then put in a circle, one group facing the other. We sat down, and the leader led us in an introspective meditation. Then it began. Forty people were going to ask me the same question several times in a row: "Who are you?... Thank you...Who are you?...Thank you...Who are you?" it went on for two hours. At first, I answered quickly and proudly: "A man... A father... Marc-Antoine... A son... A brother... A boss... A lucky man... A privileged man..." etc. Soon I ran out of labels and started repeating myself. The longer it went on, the more I realized the futility of my answers. The silence imposed itself before more truthful answers came to my consciousness: "I am the one who thinks, the one who observes, the one who...," then came: "I am stardust, an image of God, a drop of water in the ocean of love, nothing, everything, a vibration, a breath, a soul on its way." The words spilled from me like a benign confession. My ego was dissolving and giving way to something great, powerful, and perfect. I felt light, detached, and full of love for a few days. But it didn't last. My normal self returned as soon as I got back to normal life.

But over time, I discovered a simple way to reconnect with who I really am. I started by identifying all the people who have significantly influenced my life, and I created a chart with all their portraits. I came up with fifty two masters, among whom we find great sages like Jesus, Buddha, Padre Pio, Gandhi, Mandela, Martin Luther King, Sadhguru, and Om Swami, as well as some of the souls I encountered every day like my grandparents, my parents, my brothers and sister, my wife, my children, and my pets.

I also included some of the cultural heavyweights who were part of my life like John Lennon, Mohammed Ali, Cat Stevens, Sylvia Kristel, Che Guevara, Paolo Coelho, and Aldous Huxley, to name just a few. I placed this photo frame in my meditation space and began connecting to the quality that each person represented for me. The more I sat, the more I realized that each of them was a mirror of a part of my being. They offered me the opportunity to understand who I was too. Of course, their ways of expressing their truths are purer and more accomplished than mine, but they show me parts of my inner self. I invite you to do the same with your masters and let all their insights connect you to who you really are.

Another way to discover yourself is to follow this exercise. It is best to have someone you trust with you to assist. This person needs to be calm and ask questions in a clear, neutral voice. Most importantly, they should remain stoic when you reach the resistance stage.

1. Sit down at a desk with a blank paper and a pen.

2. Take a moment to clear your head. Close your eyes. Take a deep breath. As you breathe in, say, "I am in the truth." On the exhale, say, "I am letting go of my fears and ego." Do this at least three times.

3. Write the question: "Who am I?" at the top of your paper. Take a moment to reflect and write down the answer that comes to mind... Please, stop reading and do the exercise now!

4. When you are finished, breathe again, think of a second answer to that same question, and write it down. Please don't skip this, as you must stay focused on your second answer before continuing the exercise!

5. Now..., again, breathe, think, and write the third answer to that same question... I know it may surprise you but go back to your paper and answer!

6. And now, breathe calmly. Stay focused on this exercise and write the fourth answer to that same question... You may feel like giving up at this point, but please don't. This is when the work gets fascinating. Let the emptiness, the doubt, and the deconstruction of already-known ideas settle in. Dare to find a more profound answer!

7. When finished, write the fifth answer to that same question... Yes, one more time.

8. And finally, take the time to write your sixth and final answer to that same question... don't rush and go deep into your profound wisdom.

9. Once you are done, reread all of your answers until you understand them. I encourage you to write without worrying about grammar or syntax. Accept the fragments of whatever sentences you produce as they are and sleep on them. You can write them out so they're more readable later and leave them somewhere you can see them for a while, maybe in your room or at your workplace. Don't rush to finish and find the perfect answer. The most important thing is to feel who you really are.

You might want to stop this exercise around the third or fourth answer. Some people find this exercise funny, if not silly, but after stating, confirming, reinforcing, and expanding upon your already-known responses, you will step out of your comfort zone and hit a point of resistance. If you honestly persevere with the answers and go beyond this point, you will enter an area of evolution and truth. It starts with hesitation, proceeds through the deconstruction of old answers, and finally brings you to the essence of who you are.

Honor Your Ancestors

I am not a genealogist, but I feel a kinship with anyone who feels compelled to discover where they came from. In my case, I can trace my lineage back to my tenth ancestor, Christoph, born 294 years before me. He walked 130km and crossed the Bernese Alps to settle in Varen at the foot of the Leuk Valley. I don't know what drove him, but it certainly wasn't the lure of money because my family went back up the valley and settled at 1400m altitude in the cold and harsh territory of the mountains, staying there for almost 200 years.

My grandfather also came down the mountain in search of work and pretty much walked the "Tour de France" to become a cabinetmaker and carpenter. He, too, spent years on the road before returning home to marry and launch his own business. These stories of wandering and entrepreneurial spirit resonate with me. They are in my genes and they will always run through my veins. My father was the same, and that's maybe why I was able to settle 9,000 km from my birthplace.

Knowing where we come from helps us to understand certain characteristics of our behaviors. Deep-rooted experiences are repeated through generations and are the seeds of family belief systems. Listening to the stories of elders is a beautiful and gratifying sharing experience that I encourage you to do while your parents are still alive.

Make Friend with Death

I must have been eleven years old when I started looking in my bathroom mirror and saying to myself, "I want to be big." This was not a spoiled child's whim. This statement conditioned my future and was formulated from a deep, powerful, solemn space. Today, I am four inches taller than everyone in my family.

I had other moments when I saw myself having or being something else. First, in my emotional relationships, where I always imagined the profile of my subsequent conquests, then in my professional projects, where, as time passed, I knew how to express my intentions in concrete terms.

When I decided to take over management of the family business, I listed about twenty smart objectives on an A4 page and put them in a drawer. Six years later, when I was moving my office, I came across this list again by chance and was surprised to see that I had achieved all of my objectives, even though I had completely forgotten about them. At forty-two years old, when I was going through a phase of doubt and trying to figure out what I wanted to do with my life, I let myself be guided in a visualization that would project fifteen years into the future. I had seen myself at the seaside as the kind of wise man people come to meet to find their answers. Twenty years later, I live on an island by the sea and assist leaders to respect themselves fully.

The famous law of attraction states that by focusing on what we want to achieve, we will emit positive energy to attract those achievements. This concept is a current practice in sports where for example, downhill skiers will visualize their race before the competition, and the results prove that it works. We also use this in business when we define our vision statement, but for many leaders, it's just a paper exercise, wishful thinking that's quickly forgotten.

When I ask myself, "Where am I going?" my spontaneous answer is, "Towards death, like everybody else." It's not a very appealing idea to dwell on but it's a real motivator if you think about it.

Do you know why we say: "Rest in peace," when we are honoring the dead? It first appeared on tombstones sometime before the fifth century and is a prayerful request that the soul of the deceased should find peace in the afterlife. I find it interesting that anyone should ask for peace at a point when all prospects of changing anything have already passed. Why not do this when we are alive and reach serenity before we depart this existence?

Imagine that you will die in a few weeks. What will you do with your remaining days? Once the shock of the announcement has passed, you would probably only do the things that mattered to you, like reminding your nearest and dearest that you love them, thanking everyone who has helped you, asking for forgiveness from people you have come into conflict with, and eventually, like in the movie "The bucket list," doing all the things you never got round to.

Bronnie Ware, an Australian palliative care nurse, has revealed the five most common regrets of the dying, and I would like to reiterate them for you here:

1. I wish I had dared to live the way I wanted to and not live the life that was expected of me.
2. I wish I had not worked so hard.
3. I wish I had summoned the courage to express my feelings.
4. I regret not staying in touch with my friends.
5. I wish I had allowed myself to be happier.

A conscious leader must set out a compelling vision for his venture, making sure that it encourages people to be themselves, find a proper work-life balance, share feelings, and thrive.

Express Your Purpose

I wanted to be a clown and a lawyer to protect others and make my life more pleasant. This unconscious need led me to make all the decisions I did without my knowing it. It wasn't until my forties that I was invited to formulate my purpose, and it took me five more years to define it clearly and live it consciously. I know now that I am on earth to recognize the Light in the eyes of every being I encounter. To do this, I have many solutions and tools. Each time I live my purpose, warm and sweet tears flow from the corners of my eyes. They are the tears of love that I shed when I encounter this Light that unites us all. I feel tremendous gratitude and humility as I stand in awe of the great magic of Life.

As each of my two kids became young adults they both struggled to express their purpose. I pushed each of them to define what they are here for when I should have encouraged them to find their own paths and then stepped back, even if that meant letting them make the worst mistakes of their lives.

Defining our purpose is a process that needs time. I believe that our reason for being is built into us very early on. Some say that we come to earth to fulfill a mission that was decided before our birth. This idea is exciting, but no one has yet found proof of it. Nevertheless, I have noticed that many children express great truths between the ages of three and eight. It is probably during this period that we unconsciously develop the criteria for our happiness. The following years will allow us to validate our choices; like all learning, they must pass the test of suffering. It is in the darkness of night that we see the light best. During failures, breakups, confrontations, and other unpleasant experiences, we will discover what makes us peaceful, joyful, humble, grateful, and loving. Going through these experiences proves the uniqueness of our service and presence. "You can't connect the dots looking forward, you can only connect them looking backward," as Steve Jobs put it.

As leaders, we must have a clear understanding of our purpose. It must be ambitious, and we must embody it consistently. Do that, and talented young employees who are looking for a significant cause to get behind will offer you their commitment and be happy to persevere with it.

Understanding and embodying this purpose is a task that cannot be delegated. It can be co-created with the management team to facilitate their buy-in, but it must be in integrity with the group's leader. Whether sparked by profoundly moving personal experiences or a conscious and compassionate choice, our purpose must be something that takes us and future generations into a more inclusive and sustainable world.

If you are with an established company, you might want to follow these steps to validate or rephrase your purpose.

1. For two to three weeks, write down the professional actions that fill you with gratitude, fulfillment, and serenity. Ask a few key people close to your stakeholders to do the same. Make sure these actions serve a common cause. Review them and identify the type of actions that happen most regularly.

2. Ask five to ten key customers and colleagues what makes your company unique in their eyes or what kind of specific help they receive from you. Try to identify stories that touched them emotionally and list them.

3. Ask the founders and longest-serving employees at your company about their most memorable moments working there.

4. Find the common features of these stories and create a summary of five to seven of the most important ones where you identify the uniqueness of your company in serving others.

5. Take the opportunity to tell friends, their kids, and strangers a story that starts with "Once upon the time, there was a company whose aim was to (effect) (someone) by (unique actions)" and ask them to rephrase the effects and actions that have touched them the most.

6. Identify the story that creates the strongest emotions and others and is also most aligned with your own truth.

If you recently started your venture or are planning to define your purpose, here is another approach.

1. Gather magazines that interest you and that touch on various themes, then cut out images that touch you.

2. Sort these images to eliminate duplicates and pin them on a wall or the floor so you can play with them for a few days to find an arrangement that works for you.

3. When finished, take a picture and print it out in the largest size possible. Put it in your bedroom, bathroom, and office. Look at it for a few days, gradually add words, and create a story connecting the images.

4. Take the opportunity to tell friends, kids, and strangers a story that starts with "Once upon the time, there was a company whose aim was to (effect) (someone) by (unique actions)" and ask them to rephrase the effects and actions that have touched them the most.

5. Identify the story that creates the strongest emotions in others and is most aligned with your own truth.

Your Strengths Are Your Values

> You only understand the true value of happiness when you hear the sound it makes when it closes the door.

—Serge Tschopp, my father

Like the mountain climber who wants to reach the summit, I wanted to reach the heights of happiness, but I was never fully satisfied when I got there. Each time I achieved something that I thought would make me happy, it didn't, and I realized that I had created my own misery.

At the beginning of the last century, there were only a few territories left on earth for explorers to test themselves against and the South Pole was one of them. Roald Amundsen, a Norwegian adventurer, was the first to reach the Pole on December 14, 1911, after only 99 days of walking. Two other explorers were aiming for the same goal. The English captain Robert Falcon Scott succeeded 33 days after Amundsen but died with his men on the return journey, and Sir Ernest Shackleton would never reach it despite three attempts. He would spend almost two years stuck on the southern ice doing everything to save his crew, and yet today, Shackelton is the one who's best remembered, even though he failed. Unlike Scott who sacrificed his life in pursuit of his goal, Shackleton was a kind, thoughtful, and tenacious leader. When a man lost his gloves, Shackleton insisted that the man took his. When a chronic malcontent felt ill, he invited him into his cabin to nurse him. To avoid boredom, he would assign novel activities and encourage collaboration between his companions even though his ship had been stuck in the ice for several months.

Shackleton's story showed me that living according to my values is more important than achieving some lofty goal.

So, what do you value and enjoy doing most? If you don't know, I suggest trying two approaches to help you find out.

The first measures your character strengths. These positive parts of your personality make you feel authentic and engaged. There is a test that helps you to prioritize 24 strengths and you can find it here: http://www.viacharacter.org.

The second approach is to relax and think of three or four moments in your life when you felt fully energized. Take the time to think about them in detail. What did you do? What was the environment like? What did you enjoy most? Who was with you?

With your memories in mind and without thinking too hard, read through the inventory written in brackets below. Begin by underlining 10-15 verbs (or words) that represent you, challenge you, fascinate you, or that you feel strongly about.

1. VENTURE (Risk, Experiment, Go into the unknown, Speculate, Strive to do something, Dare, Seek, Undertake, Thrill)

2. DISCOVER (Learn, Locate, Discern, Detect, Distinguish, Perceive, Observe, Test)

3. TRANSFER (Educate, Prepare, Inform, Instruct, Elevate, Enlighten, Explain, Train)

4. CONNECT (Be present, Show compassion, Be touched, Empathize, Perceive, Be sensitive, and See with your heart)

5. RELATE (Be bound to someone, Unify, Link, Be part of a community, Be integrated, Be part of a family, Be emotionally connected, Be with)

6. MASTER (Do things right, Be an expert, Be superior, Set the standard, Be the best, Strive for excellence, Have primacy)

7. FEEL (Live one's emotions, Be radiant with health, Let one's energy flow, Experience one's feelings, Feel good, Be in harmony with one's body, Be in tune with one's senses, Live one's sensations)

8. CREATE (Imagine, Conceive, Invent, Assemble, Synthesize, Be original, Build, Innovate, Transform)

9. CATALYZE (Stimulate, Generate impact, Encourage, Energize, Coach, Change, Modify, Moderate)

10. CONTRIBUTE (Serve, Assist, Facilitate, Provide, Enhance, Strengthen)

11. LEAD (Commit, Guide, Persuade, Inspire, Influence, Commit, Envision)

12. HAVE FUN (Seek pleasure, Be lively, Be full of happiness, Play games, Engage in sexual play, Laugh, Play sports)

13. SEEK BEAUTY (Live gracefully, Be attractive, Look beautiful, Charming, Be noticed, Be elegant, Live tastefully)

14. BE SPIRITUAL (Have faith, Be conscious, Be in a relationship with God, Honor, Devote, Be awake, Access wisdom, Be religious)

15. WIN (Be result-oriented, Triumph, Accomplish, Acquire, Obtain, Overcome, Prevail, Earn, Gain, Succeed)

Select your five to seven most essential verbs or phrases by circling them. You will now have your key actionable values. Benjamin Franklin defined thirteen virtues to guide him on the path to personal perfection and he evaluated them in a journal throughout his life. He could never live them fully, but he constantly evolved his actions to be as consistent with them as possible. Few of us have Franklin's level of discipline, which is why I like a concept from Sufi philosophy that says if you choose one value and adhere to it fully, then the others will follow automatically.

If you want to prioritize your key actionable values, I suggest the following:

- Put two verbs in a situation and compare your activities, telling yourself that you can only choose one.

- For example, let's assume you have chosen: To Risk, Learn, and Be part of a community.

- Imagine you can either venture into a new city or learn a new lesson. Which of the two activities is more in line with who you are? Let's assume "risk" is more accurate.

- Now you can either venture into a new city or become part of a community. Which of the two activities fits you better?

- If it's still "risk" you can continue with the other two activities: you can either learn a new lesson or be part of a community. Let's choose "be part of a community".

- You have now prioritized your actionable values. In the example, it would be: risk, then being part of a community, and finally learning.

- You can use them to assess your life satisfaction. Are you putting these values into practice daily? At work, can you fully express them? You can also use them to choose where to go on vacation or which job-seeker you should hire.

Your Superpowers Lie In Your Wounds

I am always interested in the stories of those individuals who achieve exceptional things, like becoming one of the best musicians, engineers, basketball players, or professionals in their field. One thing strikes me. They often talk about a time in their lives when those around them did not see their gift. Yet all of them persevered. Where did this strength and knowledge come from that drove them to continue their journeys despite the obstacles?

At the age of 17, when I told my father that I wanted to study psychology, he found many arguments to discourage me, so it took me twenty years to fully accept that I needed to study human relationships due to various questions and wounds that arose in my childhood: why did my parents not get along? Why did my brother give me a hard time? Why were some people jealous of us? Why was there war? Why was there famine? I didn't understand these things and as an idealistic child, I found them difficult to cope with.

As a youngster, I was fearful of other people and judgmental towards them because that's how I thought they perceived me. It was as if they were inviting me to observe a hidden part of myself. I resisted but eventually became aware.

Through my work, I have realized that leaders' emotional wounds often become their superpowers. I have seen a CEO, who managed to turn a difficult financial situation around because his failure as a student made him persevere. I have also encountered a multi-millionaire entrepreneur who learned the value of money after he went bankrupt at the age of thirty and a son who seemed doubly determined to save the family business because he still felt echoes of the pain his father inflicted on him when he ignored him as a child.

The conscious leader accepts that their most intimate wounds are the source of their superpowers. Mindfully acknowledging these wounds can transform our unconscious compulsions into powerful, conscious strengths. But if we don't become aware of our shadows and repurpose our suffering it will drive us towards bad choices, as it did with leaders like Hitler, Stalin, and many others.

Your Needs Are Your Priorities

Time waits for no one, enjoy every moment and share it
with those who matter to you.

—Gandhi

When I was a teenager, everything seemed possible and time moved
slowly. Today, time passes so quickly that each birthday celebration
catches me by surprise, and I finally understand why Goethe was
imploring it to stay a while longer, but it won't, of course. It is a valuable
and increasingly rare commodity, which is why we need to prioritize
our actions. The conscious leader must apportion their time, spending
the lion's share of this dwindling resource on the company's priorities.

You are probably familiar with Eisenhower's ABC priority matrix. It
lists urgent things on one axis and important things on the other. Urgent
and important things are called A priorities, important and non-urgent
things are called B priorities, and urgent and non-important things are
called C priorities.

Procrastination and pressure from others fill our days with A and C
activities. This is to the detriment of the B activities, which are the most
gratifying and are also good for our well-being. We then need to start
our days earlier to have a moment to ourselves and end later to finish
important tasks. We slowly create new beliefs that justify our misery, like
we work better under pressure or are too busy to care for ourselves, so the
stress and pressures continue to wear us down. The less time we spend
on important, non-priority activities, the more we move into survival
space. Our irritability or sense of victimization deteriorates the quality
of our relationships and we become more and more dependent on others.

For a company to succeed, it must add value and satisfy its customers'
needs. Sometimes these needs are clearly expressed by the buyer, but our
VUCA world creates permanent changes and requires quick adaptation
to evolving needs. Those who can detect latent and unexpressed needs
before their competitors can gain a significant advantage in times of
crisis.

Here is an inventory that helps identify the needs that require special attention. I suggest that you go through them and choose the three that most concern you now. I invite you to pause reading and either find your own unsatisfied needs or a customer's latent ones in the following list. Then, have a conversation with the person who could satisfy you or the stakeholders to whom you could bring added value.

Your needs for physical well-being

Restore—Move—Rest—Breathe—Smell—Touch—See—Taste—Space

Your personal well-being needs

Learning—Authenticity—Autonomy—Choice—Clarity—Competence—Growth—Creativity—Celebration—Discovery—Efficiency—Easiness—Hope—Evolution—Harmony—Independence—Inspiration—Integrity—Freedom—Order—Sense—Simplicity—Spontaneity—Stimulation—Security

Your needs for emotional or relational well-being

Acceptance—Affection—Love—Belonging—Appreciation—Warmth—Consistency—Trust—Consideration—Cooperation—To be understood—To be heard—To be seen—Empathy—Sexual expression—Generosity—Humor—Intimacy—Closeness—Comfort—Recognition—Respect—Security—Sincerity—Support—Stability—Valuation

Our transpersonal well-being needs

Beauty—Communion—Connection—Awareness—Equanimity—Faith—Gratitude—Harmony—Honesty—Inspiration—Integrity—Peace—Forgiveness—Presence—Serenity—Silence—Synchronicity—Truth

Self-Compassion Is Your Philosophy

People often ask me what the best technique is to transform their lives. It's a little embarrassing that after so many years of research and experimentation, I've concluded that the best answer is to be kinder to yourself.

—Aldous Huxley

According to psychologist Kristin Neff, self-compassion—not self-criticism—gives us the energy to grow. Being kind to ourselves inspires us to learn from failures and try again, while self-criticism can lead to giving up or denying our failures. And unlike self-esteem, self-compassion does not depend on believing ourselves to be above average. Instead, it comes from a feeling of love that welcomes all our frailties, vulnerabilities, and mistakes. Rather than setting ourselves up against others in an endless game of comparison, we find ourselves perfect and beautiful just as we are. Another significant point is that the effects of self-compassion do not disappear when things go wrong. In fact, self-compassion comes into play precisely when self-esteem lets us down whenever we fail or feel inadequate.

Self-compassion is not a passive attitude but requires practice. I have observed that those who are "happy and successful" follow routines. They start their day calmly with gentle movement or meditation. They eat a healthy diet. They make sure they do the activities that are valuable to them, seek to satisfy their latent needs, and schedule time to develop their skills. They are very aware that how they start their day can greatly influence their daily effectiveness and well-being.

I suggest you create your own philosophy of life by defining a morning and an evening ritual. During the day, identify the priority values, character strengths, and needs that you want to embody, develop, or satisfy. Be as consistent as possible with your routine and accept that you will not achieve everything. The most important thing is to get started and then keep going. Don't focus on achievements, just lower your short-term expectations. Get used to addressing your number one priority: sticking with the daily routine. Do this for long enough and the rewards will come.

Here is what I do:

MORNING RITUAL (2 to 3 hours)
1. Get up at dawn
2. Drink a warm lemon juice
3. Walk on the beach with the dogs
4. Feed the animals
5. Do 20 min of Yoga or Taïchi
6. Meditate for 10 to 45 minutes
7. Write my book

DURING THE DAY (10 to 12 hours)
1. LISTEN: Listen consciously to everyone I meet
2. CHALLENGE: Ask questions that emerge intuitively
3. SERVE: Serve anyone who asks me to do so
4. TRANSMIT: Share my awareness and knowledge
5. HUMILITY: Speak my truth without trying to convince or please
6. GOODNESS: Perform free and unexpected acts of kindness with strangers
7. PODnow®: Pause and observe the beauty of life around me

EVENING RITUAL (3 to 4 hours)
1. Have some tea
2. Share a meal with the people I love
3. Write my book
4. Play the trumpet
5. Meditate to express my gratitude
6. Read books
7. Express my tenderness

5th Step: RESPECT YOUR RELATIONSHIPS

"In the name of God Almighty!
The people and the cantons of Switzerland,
Conscious of their responsibility toward Creation,
Resolved to renew their alliance to strengthen freedom, democracy, independence, and peace in a spirit of solidarity and openness to the world,
Determined to live together in their diversity with respect for others and equity,
Conscious of the joint achievements and of their duty to assume their responsibilities towards future generations,
Knowing that only those who use their freedom are free and that the strength of the community is measured by the well-being of the weakest of its members,
At this moment, adopt the following Constitution."

—The preamble to the Swiss Constitution

I had expressed my desire to take responsibility and was appointed as general manager. I knew nothing about the business nor about being a manager of other people. Until then, I had managed myself, and my bosses recognized my commitment. Suddenly, I became a leader and wanted to be exemplary. I worked from 7 am to 10 pm, but I had to realize that my solo efforts would never be enough. I had to motivate all the employees because our numbers were in the red. I spoke to them individually to convey the urgency and appeal to their sense of duty. They looked at me with docile expressions while sharing their difficulties.

I took on their pains and tried to answer their problems with my solutions, but the results were slow in coming, and everything that went wrong was never their fault. The computer system was not optimal, the suppliers needed the right products, our prices were too high, the customers were too demanding, and colleagues needed to be more competent. I felt that the source of the problem lay elsewhere, but I did not yet dare to ask the real questions that needed asking, and nor did I have the experience to recognize that old wounds were not being healed. I naively waited for others to share their deep needs, but were they even aware that they had them?

As we saw in the previous chapter, identifying what is good for ourselves is already an enormous life task. Discovering what is good for others is impossible if they are unaware of their needs and don't know how to express them mindfully.

I know that rules must be created to make a group of individuals function because we must avoid the effects of weak links, those who do not serve the common good and behave according to their ego or survival space. This is the difference between law and conscience. The law imposes restrictions and requirements on people so that they do the right thing. Conscience serves those who seek to connect to who they are and implores them to behave naturally, ethically, and abundantly.

As leaders who focus on respecting others, we must be aware of two significant challenges. First, discovering what is suitable for the other person is very difficult and is a common source of misunderstandings. The only way this will work is for the other person to know what he wants and to communicate it precisely while you remain fully open to receiving his messages. This requires excellent listening skills, letting go, and patience, qualities that are difficult to practice in a stressful world. It is easier to force your views upon him. Filled with good intentions, many decide what is suitable for their children, partners, employees, clients, fellow citizens, and anyone else whom they have power over. It creates conflict within families, teams, and other well-intentioned groups. For this to work, they must impose rules, such as:

- the patriarch or the elders decide
- women are at the service of the family
- children should show respect, follow instructions and stay silent
- the family or the community comes first
- Variations of these rules are also found in traditional businesses:
  - the boss decides (and is in charge)
  - middle management is at the service of the company
  - employees must do what they are told
  - the company competes with others, and we must win.

The second challenge we encounter when respecting others is that things don't change rapidly, everyone stays in their roles and they don't challenge the existing order. Unfortunately, as disruption and uncertainty increase, we see more and more polarization and misinformation, allowing abuse of power at all levels of society. Vulnerability challenges alpha-type leaders who can become disrespectful and irresponsible, provoking them to reject traditional authority. It pushes these rulers to set up repressive or controlling forces to implement complex and difficult-to-enforce laws.

To avoid a vicious circle, I prefer to focus on the relationship rather than on someone else's needs. I don't speak of "respect for others" in my PODnow® formula, but I mention "respect for our relationship with any being." That is, doing everything possible to make the space between others and myself as pure, safe, secure, and respectful as possible. We are both taking care of our own happiness. Between us is an area of communication where we express our needs and are heard. Through these exchanges, we create something more ethical and just that addresses everyone's needs. We collaborate and co-create together for abundance, each acting with freedom and compassion.

Honoring the encounter or relationship means recognizing that the other person is responsible for their own happiness, just as we are. Admitting that we are all responsible for our journey and showing confidence that everyone is capable of managing theirs too, is an act of love and encouragement. It shows that we are doing our best to move toward the joy, connection, freedom, and serenity we all seek.

With this focus in mind, it frees us from an impossible task. It becomes easier to lead while remaining calm and humble. We can listen without feeling attacked or not respected by others' comments and needs. We can truthfully follow our intuition, reveal our vulnerability, admit our mistakes, and accept the consequences.

Strengthen Your Happiness

Psychiatrist Robert Waldinger, the director of the Harvard Study of Adult Development, found out what criteria or conditions make some people live happy, long, and healthy lives. Although our society places a great deal of emphasis on financial, social, and professional success, the study has proved time and again over seventy five years that the people who do best were those who were interested in relationships, family, friends, and community.

Several studies have proven that passive loneliness that is, being alone without really wanting to be, interferes with good mental functioning, sleep, and well-being. These dysfunctions significantly increase the risk of illness and death. In the working environment, the conscious leader should identify lonely employees and create simple teambuilding exercises to help them bond with other team members.

A relationship's quality depends on our trust in a person. The conscious leader respects that everyone is free to think about what is right and good for them. He shows reciprocity by ensuring that the space for listening and speaking is fair. He allows moments of silence and integrates differences of opinion with his points of view. He thinks and speaks for himself but always with everyone else in mind.

Integrating stable and supportive relationships into the working world may seem unrealistic because most employees change jobs regularly, and bringing new blood into a team that has gradually settled into its comfort zone is often beneficial. Furthermore, loyalty is only sometimes correlated with performance. Nevertheless, the conscious leader must prioritize the cultivation of lasting relationships and ensure that employees continue to evolve by offering them regular on-the-job challenges and opportunities.

We are social animals like ants or bees, interconnected with everything around us. We depend on each other to maintain balance, so when we are alone, we lose perspective and our health suffers because our ego still requires us to be relevant to others. Our science and technology give us the illusion that humans are superior to other species, and to some extent, we have managed to bypass evolution by ensuring the survival of even our weakest members.

However, little by little, we have separated ourselves from our environment, guided by personal needs and aspirations. This has led to fragmentation and disempowerment at all levels. Success in the eyes of others, money, and "material" well-being guide our choices. We have become so disconnected that many give themselves the right to exploit Nature without concern for the impacts on future generations. Instead of relying on natural and sustainable solutions, we become increasingly dependent on artificial human constructs. Most social institutions in the so-called "developed" countries are on the verge of collapse. Our cities are filled with single people and broken families. Our egos have grown so large that we firmly believe our personal well-being is independent of the well-being of those around us. Although our physical health has improved in terms of longevity and freedom from common diseases, our emotional, mental, and spiritual health has weakened. Our food is becoming so "controlled" that it generates more complex and virulent viruses. We are so separated from who we really are that we are losing our sense of respect for others, our understanding of awe for the mystery of life, and our sense of belonging to something greater than ourselves.

Here is a small test to evaluate the quality of your relationship with someone. Pick a person you frequently interact with and rate your conversations with them from 1 (not satisfied) to 10 (totally satisfied) on the following affirmations:

In our exchanges...

1. I freely share whatever I want.
2. I am really listened to.
3. We leave moments of silence between what we say.
4. Neither person tries to prove that they are right and the other is wrong.
5. I learn something and improve my self-knowledge.
6. I see the other person as my equal.
7. We work together to serve a common purpose.

I strongly suggest sharing your results with the person concerned and thinking about how they can help you to improve your relationship.

Give Your Trust First

A relationship is like a lake between two people. If we throw a small pebble into the calm water, the ripples it causes will reach the opposite shore. If, on the other hand, the surface becomes choppy as it would in a storm, even the waves from the huge rock we lob into it will go unnoticed by the person on the opposite shore.

Just as silence is the condition that allows music to exist, so trust is the essence of constructive relationships. To explain this, I like to use the analogy of a bank relationship. If I want severe financial support, I have to offer something in return. It will depend on my guarantees and something more. The goodwill that my past actions have gained and a belief that my future actions will bring similar results. They are emotional values, impossible to measure in absolute terms but easy to evaluate when compared to others.

When you think about the people you trust the most, they will probably be family members or friends, which is expected because they are the ones you've had the most pleasant emotional experiences with. Now, list them in order of priority on a piece of paper. Put the people you can ask anything of and be completely vulnerable with at the top. You can certainly do this quite easily and assess the level of trust you have in them compared to others, but I doubt you can measure exactly how much trust you have in any particular individual.

To assess that, we need to look at where our trust in others comes from. I think there are five levels of trust. The first three emanate from the survival space, and the next ones occur naturally when we are in abundance.

1. Similarity

Have you ever been to a foreign country and met someone who speaks your language or, better yet, who comes from the same region as you? Have you not felt a spontaneous surge of connection and the desire to share everything with this person? Any animal trying to survive feels confident when it finds more of its own kind. It feels safer, surrounded by its fellow creatures. This is the first level of instinctive trust that becomes exaggerated in times of uncertainty. For instance, extremists of all stripes bind themselves together with their own distinctive signs and rituals. They demonize their opponents and blame them for their misfortunes. The more threatened they feel, the more they justify violence.

2. The dominant alpha

Animals that gather in packs will always follow one dominant individual. This male (which it seems to be in most cases) gets privileged access to resources such as space, food, and females. To be elected, they must earn their rank with horns, beaks, growls, or parries, and will remain on the throne until an upstart usurps them.

We may not think of humans as pack animals, but some of us will follow self-confident, daring leaders and use simplistic protective affirmations to justify their alignment with them. These followers are not confident in themselves and often feel victimized, so they look for others who they can hold responsible for their situation. More obedient people will follow legitimate authorities, such as a boss, a government, or a military figure, without challenging their decisions.

Our history is filled with leaders driven by these two confidence levels. Convinced of their beliefs and omnipotence, Hitler, Stalin, and other dictators used war rhetoric to motivate millions of humans to eliminate other humans.

3. Blind trust

People who dislike conflict and strained relationships blindly place their trust in authority figures. Rather than doing their due diligence, they trust anyone who knows how to hide behind a mask of respectability and they may end up being taken advantage of and consequently trust almost no one.

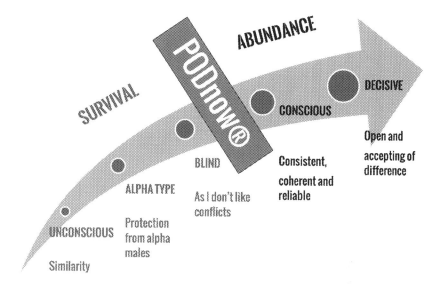

CHART 9: Five Levels of Trust

To grow in times of tension and access constructive trust, we need to get out of survival spaces by practicing the *PODnow® formula* or by using the **compass** described in the previous chapter.

4. Conscious observation

Think about people who are not in your immediate circle. Which of them do you trust? What do you think of your banker, your doctor, your priest, your colleague, your boss, and members of your government? All of them should deserve your trust, but we trust certain professions and institutions less and less thanks to widespread bad publicity. These days we are only willing to trust someone if we can observe them over time and assess their predictability, consistency, and reliability, and these are usually the criteria we use when we are deciding whether to assign additional responsibilities to people or offer them promotions. *Show us that you're reliable and have the right skill set, and we will trust you.* Human Resources appraisal systems, procurement procedures, and corporate governance help us to assess people objectively, but it begins with trust.

5. The decisive act

Think back to the most intense moments of your professional career when you learned a lot, worked long hours, and felt you were doing something important. Maybe someone had enough confidence in you to offer you a new role, let you lead a new project, or try at something where others had failed, even though they knew that you didn't have all the required skills. On paper, you didn't appear qualified, but they saw something in you and wanted to give you a chance to shine.

Many people get their big break this way. When someone you respect shows confidence in you it gives you wings. This fifth level of trust requires that the person who trusts you first has high confidence in themself. This is the attitude of the conscious leader, who allows others to learn by making mistakes and remains confident despite these hiccups. Such strength lies in their ability to anticipate failures and to provide a regular and benevolent presence for their protégés. Making this choice is easy when we share the same purpose and values. With the turbulent times we live in, our role as conscious leaders is to make sure this is the case, to give our trust first, and to maintain it while the outcomes are uncertain.

Smile Authentically

The first message of peace we give to a stranger is our smile. This expresses our sympathy and immediately takes us out of survival space. However, if the smile is not genuine, the other person will suspect that it's dangerous.

To smile sincerely, remember that life is one big theater. Hindus speak of Karma and Drama. When we know how to "turn" dramatic stories into positive ones, our compassionate and deeply truthful smile becomes natural.

A simple way to smile and bypass our survival reaction when things are not happening the way we want them to is to make four assumptions. The first is that of common sense, the second is that of drama, the third is that of the absurd, and the fourth is that of positivity. Here are three examples to illustrate my point:

- I have just been passed by a car going at high speed. My common sense tells me that this is dangerous and that the other driver could have caused an accident. My dramatic ego paints the driver as a selfish person who will soon kill himself and others if he keeps driving like this. My inner clown imagines there is glue on his shoe so the throttle is now stuck open. My positivity reminds me that when I had to take my ailing father to the hospital I drove just as fast.
- I just learned that one of our high-potential managers has left to work for a competitor. My common sense tells me that we have lost an essential talent. My dramatic mind imagines that his boss is responsible, and his teams must be demoralized. My clown sense sees that our competitor is desperate and that this is the beginning of the end for them. My positivity tells me that we need to be more aware of our key people and make sure they are aligned with our purpose and values.
- The taxman comes to check on me, and I risk a receivership. My common sense tells me to get a lawyer and a chartered accountant to accompany me. My dramatic mind tells me that it will cost me a lot of money and that they are coming after

me because I am a small guy with no political connections. My prankster mind whispers to me that they have the wrong person or that it's a hidden camera prank. My positivity tells me I will be in good standing after this audit, and I will sleep even more peacefully once I get past this somewhat unpleasant ordeal.

Communicate Unconditionally

> There are only two ways to live our lives. One as if nothing is a miracle. The other as if everything is a miracle.
>
> —Albert Einstein

As I mentioned before, we know that speech is silver and silence is golden, and that it's why nature gave us two ears and one mouth. However, finding a space for silence has become complicated today, and it's rare to find someone who can offer us a genuine listening ear.

Compassionate listening means putting all our presence at the service of the other person: our ears, our eyes, our sense of smell, our mind, our gut, and especially our loving and caring heart. Our non-verbal language is entirely open. Our brain remains calm. Our soul is at the service of the relationship.

Hedy Schleifer, a relationship psychologist, taught me how to "bridge the gap" between the person needing our guidance and us. She uses the metaphor of the city or town we live in. We know some of its streets and neighborhoods well, some not so well, and others not at all, and we may find them scary. The idea is to discover all the communities that live in the place we inhabit. In the case of a working relationship, these places are new customers, projects, solutions, strategies, etc. To do this, we need a guide, especially to visit the places shrouded in darkness that we haven't been to since childhood because we had traumatic or unpleasant experiences there. As a guide, we don't need to know these areas. We are more like reassuring friends they feel comfortable walking with because we encourage, support, and wait for them but never judge or advise them.

As leaders, we are used to expressing our vision and giving orders. We direct, orient, and guide others using evaluations, commands, and reprimands. All these actions require our words or gestures. Anyone who wants to be more productive needs feedback—those who wish to empower others need to use their ears. The goal is twofold. We first need to understand the other person's reality before co-creating original solutions. And if we want the other person to listen, we must set an example. I know you have probably heard this many times, but I have noticed that we all fall for it, especially when we experience turbulence and rapid change. Urgency activates our directive leadership style and encourages us to return to old thinking patterns. But this is precisely what we should not do. We must remain calm, innovate quickly by relying on intuition and persevere in our choices.

When I worked for McKinsey, a strategy consulting firm, we were paid very well to analyze dysfunction and propose innovative and profitable changes, but I quickly realized that my clients didn't like to be interrogated. It's like when you go to the police to make a statement. You may have been the victim of an assault, but the questions they ask can sometimes make you feel more like the assailant.

Imagine an unpleasant situation or a complicated challenge that you are currently dealing with. Take a piece of paper and answer the following questions one after another:

1. What is the problem?
2. What is causing it?
3. Who is responsible?
4. What have you done so far?
5. Why do you think it didn't work?

Now pause and observe your emotions and thoughts. How are you feeling? Are you feeling calm or preoccupied, happy or angry? And how is your inner dialogue? Are you saying to yourself, "No problem, I can handle this situation," or "This is even more complicated than I thought, and I'm lost"?

Go back to your paper and answer the following questions one after the other:

6. What would you like to see happen if anything was possible?

7. Have you, or someone you know, experienced a similar situation in the past? How did you or they solve it?

8. What are the first simple actions you can take that will help to solve your problem?

Now pause again and observe your emotions and thoughts. How are you feeling? How is your inner dialogue? What do you become aware of when you compare how you are now to how you were after the first set of questions?

We either seek to understand the problems or we strive to create solutions. Our state of mind strongly influences how we question the other person to discover their reality. Our questions will focus on their difficulties if we are in the survival space. If we are in a space of abundance, our questions will pave the way to innovations and allow them to flourish.

The following statements help us to question appreciatively and positively:

- There is always a solution to a problem.
- We are responsible for everything that happens to us.
- Everyone has a different and subjective perception of reality.
- The language used to explain something affects our perception of it.
- We are more confident when we highlight our strengths rather than our weaknesses.
- We are more creative when we dream of possibilities than when we reflect on past experiences.
- We attract or create what we focus on.

Use Conflicts To Grow

Some people come into our lives as a blessing.
Some come into our lives as a lesson.

—Mother Teresa

Some close relatives criticized me for being too 'good' for a long time. I am generous, and they wanted to warn me of profiteers. I know these advisors paid much closer attention to their money than I did. Today their bank accounts are much fuller than mine. However, I do not regret my kindness at all. My emotional account and the quality of my relationships are far healthier than theirs. It's a choice. I know the only value I can carry everywhere is the one in my heart, not the one in my pocket.

Kindness is the ability to place the needs of others at the same level as our own and to be present and unselfish in our relationships. It is an act of kinship towards those around us. Kindness means engaging in behaviors that benefit the community, usually at some small cost to ourselves. This is a fundamental virtue of a social system that includes living with abundance. First, we give, then life or the community gives back, but not always in the ways we expect. We often receive more suitable and rewarding gifts than those we have given. This happens to me regularly in my life, and if you think about it, it probably happens in yours too.

According to Tayyab Rashid and Afroze Anjum, researchers at the VIA Institute on Character Strengths, "Good people find joy in the act of giving and helping others, regardless of their degree of kinship or proximity." I fully agree with this observation. Just look at the positive energy we receive every time we do a good deed. It can range from a simple smile of thanks from a stranger to recognition and tributes from grateful communities.

Acts of kindness are easy to offer and there are numerous ways of being kind to people: sincerely greeting someone, saying thank you, surprising a colleague and sharing with him what we appreciate about his actions, recognizing the work of junior colleagues, and bringing it to the attention of our leaders, giving blood, helping a passer-by, writing a kind word to an acquaintance, rewarding someone for ethical behavior, feeding animals, returning a lost item to its owner, offering small gifts, etc.

When pressures come from all sides, our kindness is tested, and sometimes we are overwhelmed. Conflict is a tension that arises from an opposition of perceptions, points of interest, objectives, or feelings, so it follows that all relationships necessarily generate conflicts because we are all unique. We all have different missions, values, priorities, needs, and perceptions that may impede the priorities and values of others. Conflict is the norm. Harmonious and supportive collaboration is the exception.

Try to remember a big party you attended recently. Did you notice that you only felt close to certain people? Most of the guests were indifferent to you, and maybe there were some that you had no desire to meet. They repulsed you in some way. If we keep in mind that we only see what we need to and that others are mirrors of our own qualities and defects, it seems clear that they may "activate" an internal conflict within us. These people will take us out of our comfort zone and allow us to evolve.

As a positive magnet is attracted to a negative one, we are drawn to our opposites. Nature offers us this so that we can purify ourselves and learn wisdom. The path of evolution defies our conditioning. But the longer we live in survival spaces, the more intense and destructive the conflicts will be. Remaining narrow-minded and closed reinforces our prejudices and erodes our relationships. Understanding that conflict is normal allows us to deal with it mindfully.

There are plenty of books on conflict management, and I recommend authors and therapists inspired by the work of Marshall Rosenberg, the tools developed by Kenneth W. Thomas and Ralph H. Kilmann, and the theory of dramatic triangles proposed by Stephen Karpman.

Here is a practical approach you can use in situations where the relationship is not entirely broken, and you experience this tension:

1. Take the time to pause, and above all, do not react "on the spot."

2. Condition yourself positively by writing down five to ten behaviors you appreciate in your opponent. I know this might seem strange, but bringing your mindset into the space of abundance is essential.

3. Smile humbly and share the unpleasant emotions you experienced when the tension arose (see list of emotions).

4. Ask your opponent if they agree that a conflict exists between you and if they are willing to resolve it. This step is only sometimes needed but accentuates the importance of this conversation.

5. If they disagree, invite them to think about the consequences of not acting with a question like: "What will happen if we continue to behave this way?" and explore all the positive and negative effects.

6. If they agree, work together to find the real reasons for the conflict. Take your time, as there are many good reasons but few genuine ones. Often, latent unmet needs from the past cause conflicting behaviors, and they can take time and effort to excavate.

7. Search for "win-win" solutions using the questioning technique described in the previous section, "Ask positively."

8. Set concrete goals and next steps by rephrasing decisions and writing them down if necessary.

9. Schedule one to three follow-up sessions to monitor progress and encourage perseverance.

You might experience a more complicated relationship with somebody in pain who sources their perception from their own suffering. *Narcissists* are damaged people whom you can recognize by their behaviors. They regularly belittle or devalue you. They only look out for their own well-being and do not care about others. These egocentrics constantly talk about themselves and do not listen to anyone else. They are quick to judge and do not question their own behaviors. They quickly become emotional and sometimes violent if you point out their inconsistencies or abuses. They will manipulate you by putting contemptuous words in the mouths of people you care about. They reject your gifts to show that you are never good enough for them. They want to possess you and may go through your belongings, phones, or computers to identify any action that indicates that you might be escaping them. They dissolve like quicksand when you try to have a constructive conversation. They constantly bring up the past and feel victimized by many things. They blow up minor problems into endless dramas and will blame you for them. If you try any of these tactics on them they will minimize your suffering and tell you that you're being too sensitive.

They "suck up" your energy. They will make decisions without consulting you and never agree when you propose something. They only take on the tasks they want to and then do them on their schedule, not yours. They regularly threaten to break off the relationship. Still, as soon as you try to move away, they will use anger or flattery and promises to bring you back. Most importantly, they bring out the worst in you and may cause you to question your own judgment.

If you are in this kind of relationship, I invite you to think about why you should endure these corrosive behaviors a second longer. If the situation is not improving, then, like many experts, I recommend that you quit this relationship. Narcissists consume too much of your energy and they cannot be changed.

If you decide to stay with them, I recommend you find a secure and calm space to evaluate why. If you fear the consequences, like losing your job, home, or money, that isn't a good enough reason, and you should find help to quit. But if you want to persevere with this person because doing so is in line with your purpose and values, then you are making the difficult choice of compassion and mercy, and I applaud you for it. It is a beautiful path that requires self-denial and surrender.

It puts you on a course like that of the Tibetan monks who expressed compassion for their Chinese torturers, or like Gandhi when he faced the soldiers who beat him, or Mandela when he left prison and calmed the bloodthirsty fury of his people, or Jesus on the cross when he asked God to forgive those who crucified him. I hope these references will give you some strength to persevere.

Nevertheless, whether you choose to leave or stay, you will have to practice the final aspect of your True North, which is not to expect anything in return.

Seek True Encounters

On my 58th birthday, the Universe gave me a tremendous gift; this is the story of the two weeks that preceded it.

I was invited to participate in a "Peace of Mind" retreat taught by a spiritual brotherhood called Brahma Kumaris (BK) at Mount Abu, a mountain in northern India. On my arrival, I was surprised by the number of participants who had undergone complicated life trials. They shared stories of childhood abandonment, physical violence, sexual abuse, severe and repetitive illnesses, losing loved ones, abrupt dismissal, and exile. During these sufferings, they asked God to stop their ordeal. But it was not until they "surrendered" that everything changed. They had to first let go of the desire to have things change in their favor.

After the retreat, I was going to Coimbatore, in the south of India, to serve a company in creating a climate of trust among its leaders. Thirty kilometers from there lies the Isha Center of Sadhguru, one of today's most famous Indian spiritual masters. Knowing I would be in this area, I had set aside two days to be alone and meditate at this center.

At Mount Abu, I had cleansed my mind. The day after I arrived in Coimbatore, I ate something that gave me diarrhea so I went on a three-day fast which cleansed my body. As planned, I left for the Isha center on the morning of my birthday. Once out of the cab, I walked and received a blessing under the colossal head of Shiva. I prostrated myself before the Linga Bhairavi, an exuberant expression of female Divinity. I was told that she could liberate us from the past and received her grace in the form of an Abhaya Sutra, a red cotton thread that Indian men tie to their right wrist and women to the left, and that must be worn for fourty days days for the wish expressed at the time of its attachment to be fulfilled.

Soon, I found myself in front of the magnificent temple of Dhayana Lingam, the representation of masculine Divinity. I entered the half-light, found an ideal seat, and got myself into the correct frame of mind. It was time to connect and surrender to God. I calmed my breathing, let my chakras open, focused on my third eye, then my fontanel, and tried to climb above my head energetically, but it didn't work. I stayed within my head.

The day before, I received a message from Om Swami, my master, where he shared that mantras are vectors received by Shiva or God to connect with him. I decided to recite a sacred mantra I had received four years prior from Babaji Shivanandaji, another Indian guide. I whispered it eight times but couldn't climb higher.

At Mount Abu, a participant told me that my thirteenth chakra was closed and that it would open during a presentation by a Bosnian archaeologist. I had no idea what she was talking about, but I attended a presentation on pyramids by this archaeologist. He claimed that they are antennae for communicating with God and that the frequency he measured on the top of them was twenty-eight Hertz. I must confess that he sounded a bit crazy to me, but for some reason, I latched onto the number twenty-eight and decided to repeat my mantra twenty-eight times.

As I began the last recitation, I achieved a state of clarity. I opened my eyes and saw that wall spotlights illuminated the temple. As soon as I closed them again, I heard the sound of Tibetan bowls vibrating, followed by a beautiful woman's voice singing an acapella. A harp or a guitar soon accompanied her. This music was then replaced by the beating of a shamanic drum which intensified and created a trance-like state. During this concert, I was thoroughly carried away, off into the universe like a rocket, to connect to some light. I crossed the galaxies to curl up in a soft, white space. I breathed in this pure energy. I was filled with it and then came back down, while remaining connected to it by a light beam. Little by little, this powerful, sweet sensation entered my head and settled in my heart. A sudden flash of faces came to mind, and the light beam embraced all the souls who crossed my path. It was magical and real, beautiful and simple, instantaneous and eternal, unique and shared, tender and intense.

I don't fully understand what I experienced. But it was a powerful teaching that transformed the way I see myself and gave me the serenity and confidence to accept everything that happens. Stress is energy that's there to be used. Conflicts are opportunities to grow. Trials are gifts that help us to evolve. Chaos is the path we take to change unnecessary paradigms.

As leaders, we must surrender and act consciously. We serve and thrive by letting go of our ego and basing our decisions on wisdom. We suspend our emotional reactions and destructive thoughts to create sustainable solutions by learning how to use our compass and connect to our True North.

6th Step: EXPECT NOTHING IN RETURN

I always feel happy, do you know why?
Because I don't expect anything from anyone:
Expectations always hurt; life is short.
Love your life, be happy, and keep smiling.
And remember:
Before you speak, listen.
Before you write, think.
Before you pray, forgive.
Before you hurt, consider the other.
Before you hate, love.
And before you die, live.

—William Shakespeare

Tell an employee to work without pay or the restaurant owner to feed you for free. You immediately put them in their survival space. They will either want to run away or scream at you.

A friend, who belonged to the fourth generation in a line of great hoteliers, shared the best moment of his grandfather's working life. It was during World War II. His hotel was fully occupied, but no one could pay for their accommodation. Instead of money, they used to barter, and everyone did their part. Some helped with housework, others with gardening, others offered their gifts, this one played the piano, this one sang, this one repaired furniture, this one mended embroidery. All had a role, and each one felt part of a group that supported each other in the face of a life challenge. They were experiencing abundance amid scarcity. Cooperation, co-creation, play, empathy, gratitude, forgiveness, compassion, and awareness of their freedom, all these qualities were naturally lived while others around them were experiencing excruciating suffering and destruction.

We quickly become aware during trials and significant changes— the more intense the contrast, the more influential the awareness. Just look at the stars. They shine at night but are difficult to see during the day. To expect nothing in return is to say that there is no day or night. Trials and hurtful changes are not needed to become conscious. We must develop our sensitivity of perception, surrender, and let ourselves be surprised. To use the analogy of the stars, we see them because they produce light as giant balls of burning gas. To discover other planets that could be places of life like our earth, we need sophisticated instruments, intuition, and perseverance, as was the case in 1995 when the first planet orbiting a star other than our sun was discovered.

For more than 250,000 years, humans gathered in small clans of less than a hundred members. They knew each other and they knew who played the most important roles in helping the tribe survive. They depended on their relationships with everything around them. Fire, water, fruits, plants, and animals were the primary objects of their attention. Instant gratification drove most of their behaviors, and our ancestors made decisions based on their experience and intuition. Every day they reacted to their immediate needs: eating, drinking, copulating, dominating, observing, and resting filled their days. But some of them were healers who also made predictions. Today we call these people shamans, medicine men, witches, or naguals, and they had to source their knowledge from nature, stars, oracles, and the gods, a more subtle matrix that we are still trying to understand.

Once the groups settled and grew to form villages and cities, it became necessary to keep track of certain activities, like how much water or grains had been used, as shown on Sumerian tablets dating back to 3500 BCE. More complex regulation was needed, as demonstrated by the Hammourabi code, written around 2000 BCE. The more the groups grew, the more sophisticated the power systems became to manage them. But the basic principle remained the same. Some had power while others were subject to it.

Dominion and fear are intertwined and they keep societies in survival mode. The reversal of such power is achieved through violent overthrow or betrayal. Populations can be subjugated by empire, aristocracy, feudalism, political and economic systems, royalty, slavery, and alienation. Attempts to establish egalitarian and more respectful systems began very early on. The Spartans, for example, instituted the Eunomia, the equality of the law for all, around 700 BCE. The cylinder of Cyrus, dating from 539 BCE, proclaimed the prohibition of slavery, but it was not until the nineteenth century that the dominant colonial powers finally abolished the practice, and it wasn't until 1948 that the United Nations signed the Universal Declaration of Human Rights into existence.

In terms of leadership, the stick technique (as in, carrot and stick) has probably had its heyday. In bygone times, the leader was the brains behind the operation and his main concern was to get the most out of his workers by whatever means were available, including both physical and metaphorical sticks. Little by little though, as respect for human dignity became normalized, it became necessary to create other ways to make people work.

After Taylorism, the carrot was invented, and Peter Drucker formalized the "management by objectives" approach in the early 1950s. The boss was still 'the brains', so he was the one setting the overall objectives, but he now drew on his workers' intelligence by asking them to formulate goals and action plans to reach them. Since then, we have become experts in predictive madness. Our most listened-to leaders are those who can tell us where their company will be in three to five years. I recall that in the sixteenth century, plenty of predictors were burned at the stake, so it's reassuring that we've moved on since then.

Sophisticated performance evaluation systems are reviewed regularly. Business plans are sold to financial analysts who will influence the company's share price and the satisfaction of its shareholders. This system functions well in times of economic growth, but when markets stagnate or decline and competition rages, how do you reconcile the growth and profit dreams of some with the welfare aspirations of others?

Business owners feel stressed, their eyes riveted to the end-of-month accounts, while parents have bill anxiety and students don't know if they will find a job after graduation. But at the same time, jobs and whole professions are springing up now that did not exist a few years ago. Disruptive tech start-ups are appearing all the time. Robots are replacing human labor. Some leaders are giving meaning to work and encourage workers to have fun. Some workspaces are becoming more like playgrounds. Instant virtual social exchanges between peers are routine now, but at the same time, our world is becoming more vulnerable, uncertain, complex, and ambivalent. Changes and crises seem to be happening more frequently and are becoming more violent. Leaders are often quickly ejected, and employees are more liable to resign. Waves of chaos are knocking at our doors, so we need to make courageous and conscious decisions in the face of all this.

It is time to source our choices from the right place, not from our wounds but from wisdom. Quantum science offers important insights that the conscious leader must remember. For each of us, reality is something that we construct in our minds from sense data. We also know that we react better to being inspired than dictated to. Science demonstrates that matter arises from vibrations and that physical processes are organic, interwoven, and coherent. With this knowledge, it becomes clearer how we should behave. The purpose of business is to create well-being and prosperity and to help people flourish. We must vibrate positively and coherently to influence people and our organizations' living systems. The best vibrations are the ones to be found in the void of silence and the feeling of love.

Two teams of three pass a basketball between players of the same team. One is dressed in black, the other in white. We observe them on a video and are asked to count the number of passes the white team makes. While our attention is focused on the people dressed in white, a new person dressed as a black gorilla comes and taunts us in the middle of the scene. At the end of the video, we are asked how many passes we counted. Most will have the correct number. But when we are asked if we noticed anything special, very few people would mention the gorilla. We perceive only what we are focused on.

I will be upset when I order a glass of water from someone that comes half full. If it's in a restaurant and I must pay for that drink, that's understandable. But I still get upset at home, and my child does the same. We usually have expectations about how others should act. Sometimes our expectations are explicit. "Can you get me a full glass of water, please?" Often, they are implicit, that is, unspoken and assumed. "He will see that I am thirsty and bring me a glass of water." Either way, we feel upset when our expectations are unmet. Thwarted expectations are the biggest obstacle to abundant relationships. Having no expectations mitigates or even eliminates this problem. Since we have no expectations of others, we won't be disappointed or upset no matter what they do or don't do. This allows us to stay in our space of abundance, but it isn't the only benefit.

Expecting nothing in return leaves our senses open to surprise and discovery. Think of the best parties you've ever had. Were they the ones where everything was planned, and you knew what to expect? Or were they the ones where you started without planning and let yourself be carried away by everything that was going to happen to you? When I don't expect anything, and someone brings me a glass of water that is only a quarter full, I will say thank you and appreciate the gesture.

Let's go back to the example of leadership. As soon as we hear an original idea from our staff we should take note of it and encourage them to pursue it. Although we may be used to selling our products in a certain way and a defined market, let's imagine that being open to their new approach could allow us to sell them through other channels in previously unknown markets. If trusting our staff in this way proves successful, then this empowers us going forward. When we show that we're willing to trust them, they are more likely to offer us their most radical ideas for consideration and we are more likely to benefit from the calculated risks they propose.

Expecting nothing in return opens us to abundance. Usually, when you leave your home to go to work as you do every morning, you know how long it will take you. Then the traffic gets heavier, and you find yourself stopped in the middle of a traffic jam. That's when this way of thinking becomes very powerful.

Using it means you will stay calm. You will tell yourself that you will arrive when you arrive, and you will accept that. You know you did the best you could by leaving at the usual time, but you can't hold yourself responsible for unexpected events. You will stay in the space of abundance and you can call the office to inform them of your lateness with peace of mind. You can listen to beautiful music in your car, write a nice note to someone you are thinking about, look at that landscape that you pass by every day without really taking the time to truly appreciate it, talk to the driver next to you, and meet someone new. Everything becomes possible, and you arrive at the office with a smile, full of gratitude for what life has just offered you. You are greeted with sympathy and fully engaged in your tasks.

On the other hand, if you allow yourself to be gripped by the frustration of not being able to get where you are going on time, you'll probably get impatient and angry at the traffic, the commuters, the police, the car in front, and the world in general. You'll be exhausted and annoyed when you get to the office, no fun to work with, and not very effective.

This key way of responding to events is a potent tool that brings you to your True North. To be fully in abundance is to let go of your conditioning, forgive yourself for your past actions, say thank you for daily gifts, allow yourself to be surprised by events, and offer your unconditional love to every person or creature that crosses your path.

Detach, Nothing is Permanent

Konstantinos is known in the business as a tough negotiator. A seasoned poker player, he expresses no emotion and never feels unbalanced by his opponents. He is confident in his power and ardently defends the interests of the company his father founded more than thirty years ago. Yet I saw a different man when I met him with his father and brothers. He got angry, sulked, and moralized, acting like the older brother. Debates with him were heated, and he no longer made quick decisions. One of his brothers remarked that he was getting upset over little things and that work tensions were harming their family relationship. Konstantinos knew this but he couldn't escape this vicious circle.

This kind of situation happens somewhere every day. People often feel detached when defending their group or family interests but become overly involved when operating within them. The more we feel attached to someone or something, the more it becomes a factor that can potentially overwhelm and disorient us.

When Konstantinos shared his frustration and sense of helplessness with me, I suggested he try a simple practice. Each time he became aware of playing the older brother, I told him to tell himself, "This is funny," and that he should try and find out why.

Three weeks later, he was full of joy and gratitude. At the last strategic meeting he had with his family, he surprised himself several times. Instead of lecturing, he kept quiet and observed what he found funny. The atmosphere became more relaxed. Thanks to more sincere and profound conversations, original and impactful solutions emerged. The sense of true brotherhood was regained.

My wife invited me to try a detachment experiment a few years ago. The facilitator handed us a rope and asked me to tie Patricia to the floor to ensure she could not move. During this workshop, we practiced a form of yoga that stimulates the kundalini, the powerful energy that runs up the spine and opens our chakras. As I connected with my body, contemplating my wife tied up at my feet, a very unpleasant feeling flowed through me and all my energy collapsed. I felt as if I was emptying myself and dying little by little. Yet it was not me who should have been suffering from being tied up, it should have been her!

Attachment can be very pernicious. We love our children and are so attached to them that we often identify with them. Whatever happens to them happens to us as well. At least, that's what we think. When I asked my wife how she experienced the rope exercise, she said she didn't feel much. There was some discomfort, but her life energy continued to vibrate within her. It's funny how differently we experienced the same exercise.

In the same vein, I went on a retreat to experience another powerful learning. We were told to stay still for an hour and scan each body part with our minds. After several minutes, my knees started hurting, and I longed to move. This exercise went on for eleven hours a day for ten days. The more I practiced, the more my knees became numb, and I could manage the pain. But when I focused on my right shoulder blade, I felt an unbearable pressure and wished it would go away before my next scan. It didn't and became worse, but then I started to accept the sensation as it was, without adding any judgment or desire to it. From that moment on, I began to experience bliss. I became a pure and subtle flow of energy with the sensation of floating above the floor. I learned impermanence through a technique developed by Buddha called Vipassana meditation. Nothing is permanent. Everything changes constantly. Once we accept this law of nature, we can sync with what is happening and experience flow at work. Our self-confidence increases, and we are very clear about what needs to be achieved. We become agile as we perceive feedback immediately through all our senses. Fear is replaced by joy and creativity. We radiate positive energy and generate abundance for everybody.

Detachment is one of the ultimate skills we need to embody, especially if we want to elevate consciousness. It brings serenity and connects us to profound wisdom. Learning this skill is a lifelong process. Those who accompany a dying person know this capacity is in all of us. Let us demonstrate it long before we draw our last breaths.

Here is a visualization that will help you to experience detachment. It should be done at an appropriate time and in an appropriate environment. You will connect to deep attachments, so you mustn't be disturbed for the next hour and, ideally, for the whole night. I recommend doing it in the evening in a warm, familiar place like your living room or a bench in your garden. I also suggest lighting a candle and playing quiet, rather sad music.

You will need a pen and 16 small pieces of paper, and it is best if you can be guided by someone who can read the following instructions to you calmly and slowly.

1. Write down the 16 things (people, animals, roles, objects, hobbies) that are most important in your life today, one on each piece of paper. For the people, name each one individually except your children, whom you can put on the same sheet. By roles, I mean your various professional and social activities. You can leave the pages blank if you have trouble identifying 16 things.

2. When you are finished, put the sheets in front of you and sit comfortably... Close your eyes and let yourself be guided by this visualization.

3. Relax... and imagine that you just had your medical check-up a few days ago... you are now sitting in your doctor's waiting room... observe how the room looks... maybe there are other patients... you are here to receive your results... what are you saying to yourself in your head?

4. You are called... you enter your doctor's office. You have complete confidence in him. Observe the room... the look in the doctor's eyes... how he greets you... You sit down facing him... He looks at you blankly... You sense that something is not right... You learn that your results are worrisome... Focus on your surprise... your denial... your lack of understanding... You undergo further blood tests...

5. You go home... what do you do... whom do you talk to... what do you say... what do you think about... what questions are you thinking about?... Notice your anger... where it shows up in your body... who it's directed towards... you decide to re-prioritize your life...

6. Now open your eyes... take your papers... and throw away or crumple up four pieces, the least important ones...

7. Close your eyes and imagine that you are again in your doctor's waiting room... observe your fear... where does it manifest itself in your body? ... what are the thoughts that come to you? ... You are now in front of the doctor, and his look is grave... he tells you it is serious... you only have a few months to live... observe your reaction... your dejection...

8. You go back home... what do you do?... What are you telling yourself?... You decide to reorganize your life...

9. Open your eyes, pick up your papers, and throw away or crumple four more pieces...

10. Close your eyes... you have enough energy to get out of your house and do things you've always wanted to do... do them... then find a place where you feel good... you sit down... what are you telling yourself?... You think you can't handle it anymore and have to make choices...

11. Open your eyes and discard two more pieces of paper...

12. Close your eyes... you start to feel physical fatigue... the medication makes you more susceptible to it... notice who is around you... how you behave with them... how they behave with you... you don't feel like doing things... you don't sleep anymore... you feel things are not like they used to be... you are getting weaker... but you still have so much to do...

13. Open your eyes, and throw away or crumple up two more sheets of paper...

14. Close your eyes... you are more and more bedridden... you don't want to be disturbed... only the essential things and people matter to you... who is close to you?... which objects do you still have around you?... it would be best if you made choices again...

15. Open your eyes, pick up your papers, and calmly, consciously throw away or crumple up two more pieces...

16. If this feels right for you, you can continue with the visualization. Otherwise, go to step 17. Close your eyes... you are now constantly in your bed... quite tired and often unconscious... you feel the end is near... you are going to say goodbye to your loved ones... do it... then throw away or crumple the last two sheets of paper...

17. Very calmly, with full awareness, take adequate time for yourself, and relish the inner peace within you... the profound encounter you are experiencing with yourself... detached from everything but your soul...

18. Little by little, come back to the here and now... become aware that this is only a story I told you and that it is not your reality... that this story will not happen to you... then get up... pick up your sheets of paper... and put them in a trash can or burn them while thanking yourself for being alive, healthy, surrounded by people who love you, and for being able to do the things that are most important in your life.

19. If you can, take the next few hours to be present with yourself. Don't make any life-changing decisions over the next few days. Just let these realizations sink in, and you will know what to do when the time comes.

Unload Your Backpack

We unconsciously carry old stories around with us. They pollute our relationships and weigh us down. Forgiveness is a beautiful way to unload our heavy backpacks. This process takes time and can only be done by being honest. It is about "feeling" the need to free yourself from suffering that has been with you for too long. It starts in the head. Listening to others talk about their remission or reading texts like this one. Then comes the moment when your heart is ready. In every cell of your being, you feel that inner strength that cries out for love. It's not about forgetting, tolerating, or being buddy-buddy with the author of your wounds. It is about regaining your power and your peace.

Here is an exercise to practice forgiveness. You will need a facilitator, 2twentysmall stones (or grains of rice, fruit pits, beans, etc.) to keep in two pockets or two bags for at least an hour, and an appropriate location, ideally a place in nature.

If you have the opportunity, invite others to this ritual, as the group dynamic creates a more intense atmosphere. The facilitator should slowly read the following instructions with a clear and calm tone.

1. Stand with your arms at your sides. If you are in a group, stand in a circle...

2. Please close your eyes... exhale extra slowly and let the inhalation that follows it happen naturally, do this three times... feel the soles of your feet relax and settle firmly on the ground... ground yourself in our mother earth... relax... your belly relaxes... your chest relaxes... your shoulders naturally drop... your head is upright and relaxed... your breathing is peaceful...

3. Now think of the people, living or not, whom you wish to ask for forgiveness... let the ones that come to mind emerge... for each being, take a pebble in your hand and say softly, "I ask for forgiveness for..." so that your breath blows across it.

4. Open your eyes slightly, place your pebble in the other pocket and take a step forward if you are alone, or turn and take the person's place to your left if you are in a circle...

5. Close your eyes again... anchor yourself to the ground... go through each part of your body in turn, to relax it completely... breathe calmly... think about the people or groups you regularly complain about or who criticize you, your neighbors, your colleagues, strangers, public institutions, etc... let those that emerge stay in your mind... for each being or group, take a new pebble in your hand... say softly: "I ask your forgiveness for using you to vent my frustration, helplessness, jealousy or fears," and blow your request into the stone. Take a new one for each new visualization and place the used stone in your right pocket.

6. Open your eyes slightly, place your pebble in the other pocket if you have not already done so, and take a step forward if you are alone, or turn and take the person's place to your left if you are in a circle...

7. Close your eyes again... ground yourself... go through your body to relax it completely... breathe calmly... think of the benevolent entities, physical or spiritual, your guides, your wise men and women, God, the Universe, or the name you give to that which you consider being more significant than you... remember the times when you have used them to complain or take responsibility for your fate... let the ones that come to your mind emerge... for each situation, take a pebble in your hand and say softly, "I ask your forgiveness for sometimes making you responsible for my misfortunes and doubting your love," and blow it into the stone. Take a new pebble for each new visualization and place the used stone in your right pocket.

8. Open your eyes slightly, place your pebble in the other pocket if you have not already done so, and take a step forward if you are alone, or turn and take the person's place to your left if you are in a circle...

9. Close your eyes again... anchor yourself in the ground... go through your body to relax it completely... breathe calmly... think about the people, alive or not, from whom you expect forgiveness... let the ones that come to your mind emerge... taste the physical and emotional reactions that arise in you... if this feels too intense, ask for strength from your benevolent entities, those whom you have just asked for forgiveness... take the time to welcome your reactions without rejecting what is happening in you at the moment... observe how it changes... calm yourself by breathing peacefully... then, for each being, take a pebble in your hand and say softly, "I ask your forgiveness for continuing to use you as the object of my suffering. What happened belongs to the past. I don't want to carry it anymore. I free myself from this bond by asking you to forgive me for keeping you as an instrument of my hate. I don't want it anymore. I ask for your forgiveness for giving you this power over my life. You will have it no more." And blow it into the stone, take a new pebble for each new visualization and place the used stone in the right pocket.

10. Open your eyes slightly, place your pebble in the other pocket if you have not already done so, and take a step forward if you are alone, or turn and take the person's place to your left if you are in a circle...

11. Close your eyes... anchor yourself in the ground... go through your body to relax it completely... breathe calmly... take a new pebble and think about the most crucial person in your life... the only one who matters on this planet... the one we too often forget... think about yourself... this life that vibrates within you... you will ask yourself to forgive yourself for closing your heart to the trials that life has given you... you are the one who suffered... for burying your light... that was not your intention... you did not know... now you can decide to free yourself... ... "I ask myself for forgiveness... I... ask myself for forgiveness... I... ask ME for forgiveness... thank you... thank you... thank you...", blow it into the stone and place it with the other ones.

12. When the time feels right for you, open your eyes, stay connected with yourself... move forward and go to a place that inspires you... ideally in nature... take out the stones you've blown on... look at all those pebbles, grains, or pits... then give them back to the earth by scattering them in nature or tossing them into a fire... stay in this space for as long as you need to, don't hurry to "come back"... to finish, hug yourself or if you are in a group, gather and embrace, then share your experiences if you wish.

Practice Tough Compassion

Jean-Jacques had taken over from his brother as the head of the family business. With his smile and obvious competence, he immediately surprised me with his humility. He treated each of his forty thousand employees in the same way. In Jean-Jacques' eyes, they were collaborators who were doing the best they could. One of his favorite hobbies was quickly identifying the value of somebody's work and thanking him for it. When I asked why he did this so systematically, he replied, "I motivate them because even if they are not perfect, they make a difference. My role is to recognize that and my sincere thank you is worth several thousand dollars in bonuses."

He wasn't doing this to replace the bonus payments of those who deserved them, but to supplement them. Saying thank you is a simple and powerful act. It is a human-to-human recognition. "You are doing something for the common good, and I acknowledge that you are valuable to us."

Saying thank you teaches us to see the glass half full all the time by giving us the space to focus on the positives. We see the smallest, most rewarding details, and we can share them to motivate others when turmoil surrounds us.

For some, this is natural as they were raised to be polite. For those who need to improve, I recommend doing a gratitude journal and suggest some practical tips:

- Choose a special notebook and write on the first page: "My way to be happier and more conscious."

- Be precise when you describe an event for which you are grateful

- Use a list of emotions to remember how you felt

- Focus on living beings and surprises rather than on things you received

  Please don't make it a passive routine. Write every day rather than from time to time.

In the Buddhist contemplative tradition, genuine compassion aims to find ways to promote the least amount of suffering for all. In this larger context, nodding along with someone's bigotry, bullying, or falsehoods to preserve that relationship is the opposite of compassion. It interferes with peacebuilding at the societal level, even though it may appear at first glance to be a non-violent act.

Being tough means speaking up, setting boundaries, and making uncomfortable choices for the greater good. If your boss makes an off-the-cuff racist remark or your employee disrespects a company value, being tough leads a conversation to correct these behaviors—without rancor but with conviction. Although it may be uncomfortable to invite conflict, you need to convey that while you value this person you disagree with what they have done is not in line with a common purpose or set of ethical principles.

As conscious leaders, we remain human. We understand that everyone is vulnerable and that they react according to the priorities of their survival spaces when they feel insecure or hurt. As long as their behaviors are not illegal, our role is to raise their consciousness and bring them into a space of abundance.

Use this checklist to prepare yourself for your next difficult conversation.

1. Don't react in the heat of the moment. Introduce yourself if you're talking to a stranger or ask to move to a confidential space if it's at work.

2. Take a moment to prepare yourself to identify what you value about the person with whom you will have this tough conversation and especially to identify what principles or values they disrespected.

3. Communicate the importance of the situation by leaving a moment of silence before speaking.

4. Begin by genuinely valuing the person in front of you. It is not about flattery but about recognizing qualities. This is important because it allows the other person to get out of their survival mindset.

5. Conduct a conversation about the principle or value in question to ensure that it is understood and that you agree that you want to respect it. If there is disagreement, think about the unpleasant consequences of not following it for everyone.

6. Share the emotion you felt when you witnessed or heard about the scene.

7. Calmly express the concrete facts of this scenario.

8. Let the other person defend himself and remain silent, and above all do not enter into a debate of ideas, stick to the facts.

9. Once calm is restored, ask what the other person will do to become integrated. Help him to find his solution, not yours.

10. Draw up an action plan and set the next steps to ensure its implementation.

The biggest challenge that comes with conducting such a conversation is staying grounded as emotional storms rage. When you take a stand, others may retaliate with remarks that race your heart. If you are unprepared, this physical reaction can propel you directly into your own survival mindset, where you are more likely to fall back on the old reactive rules of engagement.

In these moments, the tools you have been given come into full use. We need to PAUSE and stay present. We must OBSERVE to be factual. We need to DECIDE based on our TRUE NORTH. And we need to understand what area of the MAP each one is currently navigating.

CONCLUSION

A golden handprint was glued to the artisanal extra virgin olive oil bottle. It gave it a touch of class because the price of this extract was worth its weight in gold. The lighter the oil, the more its value. This bottle contained the result of twelve successive cascades, which transferred only the lightest part at each basin.

I believe we do the same, moving from one trial to the next to gain awareness and wisdom. The more experiences we have, the more value we can add.

I believe that consciousness is universal and natural. The more we trust this perfection, the more inspired we get.

I believe that we perceive only a tiny part of what happens. The more transparent we become, the more life energy passes through us without depositing our insecurities, anxieties, anger, and wounds.

I believe that our world and the upcoming generation need extraordinarily conscious leaders. The more we understand, accept, and heal our ego, the more impactful and sustainable our behavior.

Having followed many masters and tried them myself, I know it is not through our mental reflections that we transform and evolve. It is only through our own experiences.

You have now finished reading. It's time to apply what you've learned. Go back to your notes or the table of contents, choose one subject that triggers you, make it a goal, define one single new action that you will start performing as of today, add it to your agenda, and set up a weekly meeting with yourself over the next twenty-one weeks.

As I was writing these final words, Connor contacted me. He is a good friend and an extremely successful CEO. Over our breakfast meeting, he told me about his last business trip. "I used to have fun traveling and motivating my people, but it's becoming a burden. I know it doesn't help my staff and it's not ideal for helping me make the right decisions, but I feel bad if I don't work like crazy and get involved in the details of everything. It's what my father taught me, and it did get results, but at the same time, I don't want to end up getting ill as he did." Connor has known what his goal should be for many years. He has always wanted to be at peace, prioritizing self-care over the needs of the business, but felt guilty as soon as he did so.

I suggested that he should set a weekly five-minute meeting with himself, saying: "I decide to be kind to myself even if I don't know how to do that yet."

This is the first step, which we all know is the easiest one to make, and the challenge resides in implementing it over time.

It takes constant nurturing and care for tiny seeds to grow into trees. Ask your PA, spouse, friend, or paid professional to pressure you to grow. You will need support to practice the exercises proposed in this book. The more engaged you are and the more challenging your coach is, the more progress you'll make. You will taste the fruits of serenity, impact, abundance, gratitude, detachment, compassion, and happiness.

The six steps PODnow® formula emerged from my experiences and has served thousands in their day-to-day lives. It will help you to lead in the storm. Just:

1. PAUSE
2. OBSERVE
3. DECIDE
4. To RESPECT YOURSELF FIRST
5. To RESPECT THE RELATIONSHIPS (and not the others)
6. And to EXPECT NOTHING IN RETURN

Printed in the United States
by Baker & Taylor Publisher Services